THE WALLS OF ILLUSION

THE WALLS
OF ILLUSION

Edited and introduced by
Peter Haining

SOUVENIR PRESS

'Turn on! Tune in! Drop out!'
TIMOTHY LEARY

First published 1975 by Peter Owen Ltd, London,
under the title *The Hashish Club: An Anthology of
Drug Literature, Volume Two*
This Edition, revised, retitled, enlarged and reset,
first published 1998 by
Souvenir Press Ltd,
43 Great Russell Street, London WC1B 3PA

ISBN 0 285 63414 3

Typeset by Rowland Phototypesetting Ltd,
Bury St Edmunds, Suffolk
Printed in Great Britain by
Creative Print and Design Group (Wales) Ebbw Vale

CONTENTS

THE PSYCHEDELIC GENERATION

A Retrospective Introduction

Thirty years ago the psychedelic era was born. Although it would spread rapidly all over the world, the new culture inspired by mind-expanding drugs started in America, in particular San Francisco, the former Californian gold rush town which had already, for more than a century, good-naturedly tolerated wild behaviour and eccentric beliefs in almost equal measure. In this exemplary tradition of permissiveness, the city on the bay became in the Sixties the heart of the new psychedelic culture, the mecca for hippiedom and the birthplace of a genre of literature which has inspired and influenced young writers ever since.

A whole decade earlier, in June 1953, an enterprising young poet named Lawrence Ferlinghetti had opened the City Lights Bookshop at 261 Columbus Avenue and become the publisher and patron of a rising generation of new writers who became known collectively as the Beats. From his shop on a hill looking out towards the formidable Alcatraz prison in the bay, Ferlinghetti issued the first works by the group of men whose names would become synonymous with this literary movement: Neal Cassady, Jack Kerouac, Allen Ginsberg, Gregory Corso, along with some of his own poetry and prose. His unswerving defence of these controversial writers and their books about free love, alcohol and drugs against the forces of censorship and the establishment became legendary ... and ultimately successful. To him they were the representatives of an 'alternative' society, creating their own standards and finding their own means of expression—in the main through the use of stimulants and a drive towards personal experience of all that life had to offer, however strange or bizarre it might seem by accepted standards. The early stimulants used by this group were mostly 'pep' pills and alcohol, but they soon turned to the wider fields of hallucinatory, and in some cases narcotic, drugs with which they created their legend. The Beats were in turn the precursors of the hippies and the whole drug-inspired creativity of the Sixties which has left an enduring mark on twentieth-century writing.

Today, a number of streets in San Francisco are named after some of the best known Beats, including Jack Kerouac Street which, appropriately, runs right alongside the City Lights shop. It is an area that holds vivid memories for me: I first visited it in 1967 as a young publisher from London, and sampled the world of psychedelia and mind-expanding new literature courtesy of Lawrence Ferlinghetti. Later, I republished several of his City Lights titles in Britain and, more specifically, with his help put together this anthology. First published in 1975, it is now being reissued to meet the renewed interest in the Sixties and its culture which has been made evident by the successful republication of a number of the cult novels of the time; by the re-releasing of records by the most significant artists and groups of the day; and by the demand for period memorabilia including clothing, artefacts and posters. The popular TV series *Absolutely Fabulous* may well have found plenty of examples with which to send up the worst excesses of the era, but to those of us who lived through those days it is very far from being representative.

What has been called the 'founding text of psychedelia', *The Doors of Perception*, was published by the English novelist Aldous Huxley the year after Ferlinghetti opened his shop. But it was not until 1955 that the actual word 'psychedelic' was coined during the course of correspondence between Huxley, who had settled in California, and a scientist friend, Dr Humphrey Osmond. In trying to describe what had been experienced under the influence of LSD, Huxley resorted to poetry:

> To make this trivial world sublime,
> Take half a gramme of phanerothyme.

The last word in his couplet derived from a term relating to the spirit or the soul and this was what gave Dr Osmond his clue. Replying to Huxley in the same vein, he proposed a word from the Greek which means, literally, 'mind-manifesting':

> To fathom hell or soar angelic,
> Just take a pinch of psychedelic.

Neither the scientist nor the writer could have known that not only had they invented the label for the generation that would experiment with the psychedelics (LSD and mescaline) in what became known as 'tripping', but that in those few lines they had effectively launched the literature of psychedelia. For those who have never encountered Aldous Huxley's seminal work on drugs, an example is included in this book.

The news about 'tripping' was, in the main, spread by young writers and musicians (who were enthusiastic promoters) and the media (which was almost universally hostile). The Beatles, who played their last concert at Candlestick Park in San Francisco on 29 August, 1966, were at the forefront of this movement—in particular John Lennon—and their record 'Tomorrow Never Knows', in which Lennon chanted lyrics from Timothy Leary's *The Psychedelic Experience*, had an immediate and profound effect on pop culture. Other records by The Byrds ('Eight Miles High'), Jefferson Airplane ('Blues From An Airplane'), Big Brother and the Holding Company ('Ball and Chain'), The Rolling Stones ('Paint It Black'), The Yardbirds ('Happenings Ten Years Ago'), Pink Floyd ('Interstellar Overdrive') and The Grateful Dead ('That's It For The Other One') confirmed the arrival of a new era. The writings by those in this book established its place in literary history.

Looking back with the benefit of hindsight, it is not difficult to appreciate that the survivors of the Sixties are divided into two camps. One group believes it was a regrettable era that promoted free love, unilateral nuclear disarmament, flower power, anti-Vietnam feeling and, especially, drug-taking which they claim helped thoroughly to mess up modern life. The other sees it as a decade when freedom of expression was won, popular music was genuinely original, and there was a sense of optimism and humour abroad in the world. Fashion, food, books and lifestyles were for a time treated without overweening seriousness, but as fun. And although the words 'psychedelic', 'hippy' (a word coined by the San Francisco columnist Herb Caen in 1967) and 'underground' are irrevocably associated with the period, they have provided a legacy of literature, art and music which represents an explosion of youth culture the like of which had not been seen before—nor has it since. Indeed, several of the issues first raised in the Sixties and laughed at by many are now universal concerns: nutrition, civil rights and the environment. The one undeniable tragedy is that it should all have ended in 1969 with the killing of a fan by Hells' Angels at the Altamont Concert which brought a close to all the 'Summers of Love'.

There are, however, a few artefacts marking the days of the psychedelic generation still to be found in San Francisco. The Psychedelic Shop on Market Street continues to sell books, music and the characteristic posters of the time in the shadow of a huge representation of the 'flying eye' logo of The Grateful Dead, the group which, musically speaking, came closest to symbolising the era; while the group's tall, sombre-grey house at 710 Ashbury, in the heart of the Haight-Ashbury district, is now virtually a shrine. Some of the survivors of the Sixties rock groups even gather occasionally to play sets at places like The Saloon on Grant Avenue, where they joke to audiences about the days when, high on drugs, they believed they were going to change the world. The Golden Gate Park Stadium where, in front of more than 20,000 people, Timothy Leary gave his famous 'Turn on! Tune in! Drop out!' speech which became the battle-cry of the psychedelic generation, still embodies a lingering sense of the Sixties about it—though not so readily distinguishable as Lawrence Ferlinghetti's City Lights Bookshop.

In Britain, Beatles memorabilia from the Sixties are highly prized, and the various locations associated with them in Liverpool draw millions of tourists every year. Psychedelic posters— 'Pictures from the Stoned Age' as one newspaper recently called them—are also avidly collected and the best examples by American artists such as Rick Griffin, Stanley Mouse, Alton Kelly and Peter Max, the British duo Michael English and Nigel Waymouth, and the very influential Australian, Martin Sharp (who created the enduring images for Bob Dylan's 'Blowing in the Wind', 'The Jimi Hendrix Experience' and the poster for the 'Legalise Cannabis Rally' in London in 1967), plus the companies with their whimsical names like The Fool (who painted John Lennon's Rolls-Royce in psychedelic colours and designed the logo for the *Sergeant Pepper* album), Hapshash and the Coloured Coat, Lead Pipe Posters, The Big O Poster Company, Osiris Vision and East Totem Wheel (whose 'colour wheel posters' were the forerunners of today's 'Magic Eye' books), now fetch hundreds, even thousands, of pounds at auction.

These psychedelic fantasies, along with the music of the Sixties rock groups and the drug-inspired writings in this book, are a memorial to an era that shaped a generation. At the time they were signposts to a new space; today they are a key to the winning of the right of free expression: a fact of life too often and too easily taken for granted.

Peter Haining
London, August 1997

PROLOGUE

Brian W. Aldiss

Just as we sometimes become aware that we are in a gathering of people which consists, in effect, of few who are perceptually alive; just as we sometimes become aware—and this is the beginning of love—that we are in the presence of somebody whose thought and body can immensely enrich our own; so we sometimes wish for an awareness that transcends our own limited consciousness. The present becomes our prison. We have to escape, even if that escape means moving deeper into our selves.

Means of escape are legion; life hath ten thousand several doors for men to take their exits, as Webster almost said. This anthology concerns one particular exit: that baroque, mysterious doorway marked Drugs; and some particular people: those baroque, mysterious writers who have chosen to make their way through it.

For every writer who allies himself with a drug—for every Wilkie Collins quaffing down laudanum by the tumblerful, for every Anna Kavan on snow for thirty-five years—there are many whom the alliance destroys. Writers probably have a better survival rate than other people, since they have their writing and the objectivity it requires to keep them on an even keel. Given an element of self-destruction in their natures, they utilise the drug to present some *outré* vision of the world—a vision which ordinary mortals without the fold are prompt to recognise as one more immensely convincing version of the truth.

And why not? For a third of every day of our lives, we are out of our minds, convinced utterly by the thousand charades of sleep in which logic, time, our very selves, undergo distortions or annihilations which must make any surrealist grit his teeth with envy. Modern theories, such as those advanced by Dr Christopher Evans, suggest that our dreams may be the brain's efforts to order the events of the day, as it comes off-line like a computer after a particular programme. I believe that, further, these witty distortions of thought-power are very much the cicatrices left by man's evolution from the animal, which will heal in a few million years, as we become fully human. If this is so, then what Sir Thomas Browne called 'the famous Nations of the dead' all dreamed more richly than we. Perhaps the present-day interest in the use of drugs can be accounted for by our trying to compensate for this unacknowledged loss at a time when evolution may be making one of its gear-shifts within us.

However that may be, drugs are as old as mankind itself. Which is to say (if guessing is not cheating) that drug-induced states were there at the birth of religion, art and science, all of which spring from the same creative impulse.

Of course, a book such as this has a great deal more romantic appeal than one about, say, snuff, although we recognise that alcohol, tobacco, aspirin and so on are merely socially acceptable drugs. As we can control, at least to some degree, the effects of alcohol, so with other drugs: LSD in particular is an accomplice, a symbiote, not an assassin. It seems that the brain on occasions secretes its own psychedelic chemicals, as an aid to perception.

Certain so-called psychotic states are known to be the result of such internal dosages. Recent research indicates that schizophrenics suffer a much lower incidence of cancer than the rest of the population; what are they secreting? Or could it be that cancers originally developed to cure man's schizophrenic state? As these stories remind us, there is much we do well to be unsure about.

The stories work at doing directly what all forms of fiction do less directly: they allow the reader a freedom in charades in which logic, time, his very self, undergoes a distortion or annihilation which otherwise he experiences only in sleep. Just to take the time element—the fall of the House of Atreus can be played out before us in a single evening, or the Fall of the House of

Usher in a single hour; or, on the other hand, James Joyce's Bloom enjoys a Dublin day which may take us a week to travel. In the cinema or on TV, we can see the triumph and destruction of the Third Reich whilst smoking a couple of cigars. This element of time-distortion in art is one of its great unconscious attractions for us. In our art galleries, we find moments and scenes frozen for ever, much as

> The sweet, sad years, the melancholy years,
> Those of my own life,

as one opium eater expressed it, become embalmed in our memory.

When Aldous Huxley first took mescaline, one morning in the spring of 1953, he found himself in 'a timeless bliss of seeing'. Experiencing a complete indifference to time, he says this: 'I could, of course, have looked at my watch; but my watch, I knew, was in another universe. My actual experience had been, was still, of an indefinite duration or alternatively of a perceptual present made up of one continually changing apocalypse'.

The time factor was banished. Could this be, I wonder, the predominant reason why we turn to drugs, that they lend us an illusory immortality?

If the clock in the mind is stilled which first started when man, alone among living things, discovered death, then other faculties awake, chief among which seems to be the visual sense. (Even beer can bring its hallucinations!)

'This is how one ought to see, how things really are,' exclaims Huxley from his trance. It is the cry of artists everywhere, seeking to convince their fellow men and women of the wonder of the world, of the lies of mundane life. Always at the basis of the cry lies an implicit condemnation of the way in which the world moves too fast. We must, says the artist, stop and stare, stop and dream, or stop and drowse.

Proust, speaking of Gérard de Nerval, refers to the way in which one's life may be compressed into the few minutes before sleeping. Of these hypnoid visions, Proust says, 'Sometimes in the moment of falling asleep we see them, and try to seize and

define them. Then we wake up and they are gone, we give up
the pursuit, and before we can be sure of their nature we are
asleep again as though the sight of them were forbidden to the
waking mind. The inhabitants of these pictures are themselves
the stuff of dreams.'

And he goes on to quote from a poem of Nerval's:

> Puis une dame, à sa haute fenêtre,
> Blonde aux yeux noirs, en ses habits anciens . . .
> Que, dans une autre existence peut-être,
> J'ai déjà vue—et dont je me souviens!

There are many women, many life-styles, which would suit
us; ordinary waking life defeats them.

To conclude on a note of speculation. Drugs, by abolishing
that enervating sense of time from our minds, can give us the
chance to touch on impossible things, as these stories show; we
can move into the past, the future, or, as Nerval says, into other
existences.

A research group in the Maryland Psychiatric Research Center
in the United States discovered that LSD can help people who
are dying, particularly those who have an extreme fear of death.
For some of these patients, the LSD trip proves extremely horrify-
ing; but the importance of the experience lies with how a patient
integrates it with his previous life-experiences. In effect, he
receives a lesson in how to die (Huxley needed no such lesson,
although he went out on a tide of LSD).

The brain under LSD is in some respects – for instance, as
regards oxygenation—under similar circumstances to the brain
approaching death. So the trip represents a physical as well as a
spiritual lesson.

These stories also come from undiscovered territories within
the mind. I wonder if, in throwing up their distorted and magnified
images of life, they are not also bringing us word from the lurid
worlds of death.

1

Writing the music of life
   in words.
Hearing the round sounds of the guitar
   as colours.
Feeling the touch of flesh.
Seeing the loose chaos of words
     on the page.
      (ultimate grace)
(Sweet Yeats and his ball of hashish.)

My belly and I are two individuals
   joined together
     in life.

THIS IS THE POWERFUL KNOWLEDGE
   we smile with it.

MICHAEL McCLURE (1932–   )

The drug experimenters who are the subject of this book had their beginnings in the United States during the late 1950s, with a small coterie of writers and poets now collectively remembered as the 'Beats'. They sought an 'alternative' society by creating their *own* standards and finding their *own* means of expression— in the main through the use of stimulants and a thirst for personal experience of all that life had to offer, however strange or bizarre it might seem by accepted standards. The early stimulants used by this group were mostly alcohol and 'pep' pills, but as the effects of these palled they turned to the wider fields of hallucinatory, and in some cases narcotic, drugs.

The prime mover of this new search for experience was undoubtedly the legendary Neal Cassady; his freewheeling, amoral life-style became a pattern for that of his great disciple, Jack Kerouac, whose work made the world aware of this new revolution in its midst. While they brought 'Beat' to America, a 'spiritual brother', William Burroughs, was travelling abroad and indulging himself in a variety of drugs in a way which, while it proved intensely revealing and in the long run was to be of enormous value, very nearly killed him. Despite the importance of his writing based on his experiences, Burroughs was to open wide the most fateful new gates of perception where drug stimulation was concerned when he went to the Amazon in the early 1950s in search of the mind-expanding drug yage. During this 'expedition', he wrote regularly to his friend Allen Ginsberg, then an unknown poet living in New York, acquainting him with all his experiences. Seven years later Ginsberg was to follow much the same path in Peru; he, too, faithfully recorded his visions under drugs.

The Beat Generation were the immediate precursors of the 'hippies', and the heralds of the drug-inspired creativity in the 1960s. Their work lives on, with Burroughs and Ginsberg now acknowledged as major influences on American literature, Kerouac's books enjoying a whole new readership and Neal Cassady finally recognised – posthumously – as one of the great pathfinders in the quest for a chemical paradise.

THE FIRST THIRD

Neal Cassady

*Although, in popular mythology, Jack Kerouac has become
regarded as the 'father figure' of the Beat Generation, he owed
his inspiration to the freewheeling Neal Cassady (1920–1970).
Cassady, who features several times in Kerouac's books as either
'Cody Pomeray' or 'Dean Moriarty', was a reckless, fast-talking,
one-time juvenile delinquent, whose rebellion and search for
'spiritual enlightenment' created the Beat life-style. Born in
Denver, the child of a broken home, Cassady took to the road
when still in his teens and on the way encountered both alcohol
and marijuana. Together with mammoth, cross-continent journeys, these were to prove the main pursuits of his life, and one
biographer has referred to him as the 'Johnny Appleseed of pot'.
He wandered the American continent introducing friends and
acquaintances to the drug and, according to the American journalist Dan Wakefield, 'liked to turn on hitch-hikers in his cross-
country odysseys'.*

*In 1947 Cassady met Kerouac and the two men found an instant
affinity. For a year they were constantly in each other's company,
taking any and all drugs they could find: benzedrine, marijuana,
peyote, and gallons of alcohol. They talked endlessly—Cassady's
non-stop, stream-of-consciousness anecdotes providing the inspiration for Kerouac's early work—until the following year when
they took to the road together. Cassady was heading for imprisonment for possession of pot, disillusionment with most drugs, and
then a brief link-up with Ken Kesey and his 'acid' experiments
in California with the group called the 'Merry Pranksters'. Kerouac, on the other hand, was bound for* On The Road, *the position*

*of a cult hero and international acclaim for his writing. The
closing years of Cassady's life show that while he was always
ahead of his contemporaries in his search for new stimulants, he
lacked their objectivity and sound approach to experiment. In
the last months of his life he went to Mexico and there sought
still more exotic 'highs' using both drugs and alcohol in doses
which were eventually to prove fatal. While personal memories
of him may have faded, he lives on in Kerouac's work probably
larger and more grandly than he did in life. Of his writing very
little indeed has survived, perhaps the only really significant item
being* The First Third *which Lawrence Ferlinghetti told me is all
that remains of his 'much lost and found' unfinished autobiography. Despite the composed nature of the prose, it was certainly
mostly written while Cassady was alternating between marijuana,
benzedrine and peyote, and does show fairly clearly his stream-
of-consciousness, no-punctuation style. The piece reprinted here
is an extract from* The First Third, *describing what happened
when Cassady returned to live with his mother for a while.*

*   *   *

'Sweet and lovely isn't it . . . Careful, this is the last roach, men. (*blasting
furiously*) (*gagging, groaning*) This roach, this immortal roach, this tre-
mendous . . . Which one is the tokay? All three. This is the one you gave
me, hey? The fullest one, obviously, I've not touched it. Now this roach,
this immortal roach like a beautiful soul of some dead blossom of a rose
will plop into the muscatel, only it's tokay, flame tokay, and I shall drink
it (*laughing*) in liquid form, a concoction of, ah, doubtful, ah, qualities,
'cause you know, not being a lush type . . .'
                    'The Tape' (of a conversation with Jack Kerouac in 1947)
                                             from *Visions of Cody*

Brothers Ralph and Jack had deposited me in number 38, which
was the first apartment on the left after coming through the main
entrance off the big dozen-step-high brick and cement Snowden
front porch. It was there, an apartment poor, even by Snowden
standards, that mother, now 43, Jimmy, approaching 12, Shirley,
just 3, and I, turned 7, lived out the turbulent 1933–34 school-
year. My new home had been quite an improvement on the Metro-

politan, having a large room that was used for everything except whatever activity could be crowded into a small kitchenette; along one much marred wall of the high-ceilinged, no rug, and wainscoted living room there was beneath long glass-door cupboards an oblong wood panel centred with a handle which was pulled to bring out on its always sticking rollers a large bed we all used for sleeping—except corner palleted Jimmy and infrequent overnight visitors. It was here in the wall-bed that Jimmy would imprison me with typical care to restrain any show of sadistic delight, knowing well that a revealing chuckle or two might betray his evil to mother. When he shoved it the bed went inside the wall horizontally and my clearance was less than a foot; besides fear of this lack of room to rise up as I lay there breathing ever so slowly in total darkness, there were stronger twin terrors of realisation; one, that I couldn't scream for release or Jim would beat me, and two, that any yelling would also unnecessarily hasten the extinguishing of the all too small supply of oxygen, for I had known about the agony of suffocation ever since having once seen, with Dad, a film the plot of which had the villain, who drugged well-to-do young girls somehow, to take compromising photos for the purposes of blackmail, inadvertently though (through his own greed) locked inside one of his victim's father's banklike vaults and flailing about dramatically clutching his throat in obvious last gasp of strangulation until released in the final nick only after the hero fiancé of the photographed half-clad-languidly-lying-duped-doped-ill-used girl had managed to frantically persuade her shock flustered, vengeance-determined and naturally uprighteously anti-smut father (the only one, of course, who knew the combination) to open up for the sake of his conscience later and the police now, despite the good and moral apparent reason for letting the rascal die. And there was another thing my imagination feared whenever I laid sweatsoaked in the rank closeness of the trap which Jim would open sometimes only after hours of my quiet submission (his demeanour registering characteristic disdain that always showed contempt and hid glee): a concern over the building weight above that, although thankfully I knew Denver was not subject to earthquakes, might fall to crush me in some catastrophe such as fire. These claustrophobic experiences brought on another reaction even more unusual and less easy to explain—a reeling in my senses caused, I imagined, by an offbalanced wheel whirling around with close clearance inside my skull and which, while slowly increasing in tempo set up a loose fan-like vibration as it rotated into ever-tightening flutter; more exactly, it was simply an awareness that time, in my head had gradually apexed to about triple its ordinary speed of passage, and while this thing was happening I thought of it as just a circular flying object twirling through my mind, for lack of a better way to think about this spinning sensation, but actually *felt* it (nerve-wise) for what it was—only a strangely pleasant, yet disturbing enough to frighten, quickening of my brain's action which resisted any vigorous attempt to throw it off and return to normal-headedness: this time acceleration came and went of its own accord making me thus dizzy-minded (though only while inside my mattressed jail, and then not every time) all through this first Snowden year. It was nearly a full score years later before I again had, but this time tried to hold and analyse, similar headspins (though from much different stimuli) and found that by strong concentration I could turn this time-quickening off-and-on (for short moments) once it had started. But the prime analytic requisite—to hold still as death and listen intently for the inner ear to speed up its buzz until, with regular leverlike flips, my mind's gears were shifted by unknown mechanism to an increase of time's torrent that received in kaleidoscopic change images, clean as the hurry of thought could allow, rushing so quickly by that all I could do was barely catch one before another crowded—was much too difficult to continue for very long, since any outside distraction, such as noise, would disrupt the process of maintaining the necessary body inertia; and I failed to match these mental eruptions firmly enough, being so fleeting, to any reasonable explanations in reality, so that the cause, cure or real workings of these singularly fresh and concise visions were for-ever beyond my diagnosis, each one in fact beyond my remem-bering except as phantom residue of some flashing scene. While on the subject, I note that several writers such as Céline and

William Burroughs have mentioned mysterious fevers in early childhood which gave off similar exhilarating sensations to their mind's eye; would that medical men could adequately explain these boldly etched and racing glimpses in pre-rational children at hallucination's brink; perhaps there is a regular fever like there is, say 'the three-month Colic' in infants.

WRITING DREAMS

Jack Kerouac

Although it was Neal Cassady who inspired the Beat revolution, as I have pointed out, it was Jack Kerouac (1922–1969) who became 'the King of the Beat Generation and the Zen terror of the transcontinental blacktop', to quote Time *magazine. His wandering, his experiments with drugs, and his books—both fact and fiction—built him into a cult figure and a major influence on the life-style of the young. For all his later unruliness, in his formative years in the 1930s Kerouac was the archetypal young American, enjoying school, playing football (he was a talented player), drinking beer and going to the cinema. It was not until he went to Columbia University that the first signs of change became evident. Among the friends he made while he was there were Allen Ginsberg and William Burroughs—and the three men, with other students, began the search for the state of 'beatitude' (the word from which 'Beat' derived) which subsequently took them all on such varied and now well-recorded paths.*

Kerouac's major influence, however, was to be Cassady when, in the immediate post-war years, they sought experience through travel and drugs: Kerouac recording his impressions under benzedrine and marijuana in non-stop prose which he literally poured out into the typewriter. However, many of the references to drug-use were edited out of his earlier works by his publishers, and Visions of Cody, *his most explicitly drug-based book, was only published in full in 1970 in a generally-available edition. Kerouac found international fame when* On the Road, *his novel celebrating the wanderer, Cassady, was published in 1957, ten years after he had begun the book.*

The later years of his life were to prove equally unstable; he was less on the road but took more to excessive bouts of drinking. He was married three times and relied increasingly on his memories for his later books. When he finally abandoned the road, having become alienated from Neal Cassady who continued to live the archetypal Beat life, he took to lecturing and attempted to change his image—suggesting that the cause of his unsettled life had been a fierce independence inherited from his ancestors in Brittany. His novel Satori in Paris *is a record of his search for his predecessors in France. At the time of his death in 1969—back in his home town of Lowell with his third wife and his beloved mother—he was still attacking many of the values of society, but had found less and less compatibility with the young, referring to himself in his last published article as the 'Bippie-in-the-Middle'. When he died, his estate was valued at just $91; today it is said to be worth more than ten million. Film rights have been sold in several of his books, including* On the Road *to Francis Ford Coppola; a Kerouac CD-ROM has been authorised; and such is the interest in any artefacts relating to the author that in 1995 actor Johnny Depp paid £10,000 for his old trench coat.*

Kerouac's memory remains fresh in his works, but perhaps nowhere did he more clearly reveal himself than in the stream-of-consciousness writings which formed his Book of Dreams, *a work dating from his 'blood-brotherhood' with Cassady and their joint drug experimentation. In the extract below, 'Writing Dreams', are to be found many of the major images of his best work: the Beat life, drug hallucination, the rebellion of the young, and the eternal craving for something just beyond the horizon. Here, too, there is evidence of the perennial struggle in Kerouac's subconscious between his mother and the values of home and hearth, and Cody Pomeray, the personification of Neal Cassady, who is always beckoning Kerouac along the road of adventure, weirdness and anarchy, even to the very brink of madness.*

*　　*　　*

The dreams that accompany me are of the infinite, never-ceasing, painful, karma-activity of the discriminating brain picking up its harsh matter and tormenting out its cold subjects, which we keep calling life . . .

Essay, 1961

1

Oh! the horrible voyages I've had to take across the country and back, with gloomy railroads and stations you never dreamed of— one of them a horrible pest of bats and crap holes—and incomprehensible parks and rains. I can't see the end of it on all horizons.

Jesus, life is dreary. How can a man live, let alone work—sleeps and dreams himself to the other side and that's where your Wolf is ten times worse than preetypop knows—and look, I stopped—*how can a man lie and say shit when he has gold in his mouth?*

Cincinnati, Philarkadelphia, Frohio, stations in the Flue—rain town, graw flub, Beelzabur and Hemptown I've been to all of them and read Finnegain's Works. What good will it do me if I don't stop and righten the round wrong in my poor bedighted b—what word is it?—skull . . . Talk, talk, talk—

2

I went and saw Cody and Evelyn; it all began in Mexico. On Bull's ratty old couch I purely dreamed that I was riding a white horse down a side street in that North town like in Maine, but really off Highway Maine with the rainy night porches in the up and down America, you've all seen it you ignorant pricks that can't understand what you're reading, *there*, with sidestreets, trees, night, mist, lamps, cowboys, barns, hoops, girls, leaves, something so familiar and never been seen it tears your heart out. I'm dashing down this street, cloppity clip, just left Cody and Evelyn at a San Francisco spectral restaurant or cafeteria table at Market and Third where we talked eagerly plans for a trip *East* it was (as if!) (As if there could be East or West in that waving old compass of the sack, base set on the pillow, foolish people and crazy people dream, the world won't be saved at this rate, these are the scravenings of—a-lost-sheep.)

The Evelyn of these dreams is an amendable—Cody is—(cold and jealous)—something—don't know—don't care—Just that after I talk to them—Good God it's taken me all this time to say, I'm riding down the hill—it becomes the Bunker Hill Street of Lowell—I'm headed for the black river on a white horse—it broke my heart when I woke up, to realise that I was going to make that trip *East* (pathetic!)—by myself—alone in eternity—to which now I go, on white horse, not knowing what's going to happen, predestined or not, if predestined why bother, if not why try, not if try why, but try if why not, or not why—At the present time I have nothing to say and refuse to go on without further knowledge.

3

Digging in this woman's cellar to plant, or transplant, my marijuana—under clutters of papers (just a minute before was going thru my own things, in a huge new room)—clutters of rubber bands, etc., and digging into dirt to make plant bed, but realised how deep her hole was beneath her junk, thought to myself, 'The old lady's—the older you get the deeper your cellar gets, more like a grave—the more your cellar looks like a grave.' There was a definite hole to the left—a definite saying.

I was foraging for my stories and paper—earlier I was in a room, working for a man as secretary, he was a masquerader, a fraud—and an evil pulp magazine crook genius. My mother visited me as if I was in jail—I turned over in my bed, my cot, interested in these things—

4

A big strange war has broken out in America; about 400 or 4,000 Prisoners of War in a camp break loose and burn their way down the Mississippi towards New Orleans—the whole country gets panicky, mobilises, it seems to me to be kinda silly, it's that old grey war again only now right in our own country.

I go down to New Orleans in the general upheaval of war; at night in the great spectral glittering city I arrive at the boys club to meet everybody and there's Cody!!—and he's suddenly given up family and responsibilities and spiritually fallen apart and is a drunkard, a wino, red face and broken nose, tragic, dirty, young-old—I'm so astounded by this change and yet I think 'He must look just like his father now!' Dave Sherman, others spectrally are there too—card-games—We three go stay at a guy's house, queerlike, John Bottle—like—he doesn't expect us but that very night is having a big queer party and we are welcome—At the piano sits one of them, tall, dark, pockmarked, with a malformed hand, whom I address as '*Hands*' in requesting a tune and get a dirty look—We're in jeans, young, the queers seem to dislike us, but I don't really (in retrospect) believe they could have—and meanwhile those tragic Prisoners are fighting their way down the Mississippi leaving their dead and diminishing in numbers with every skirmish, every new broadcast.

I feel sickened by the cowardice and hysteria of America become so blind as to misrecognise the freedom needs of imprisoned men 'Communists' or not—the great pileup of arms and pathological propaganda on them. Cody is battered, nose broken, fired from the railroad, a hobo. Cody Pomeray in his inevitable final American Open Spaces Dempsey Whisky Bottle Night, as always I'd dreamed of him and myself—But now it's a serious reality and I realise Cody is going to die of wine and neglect—He doesn't talk excitedly any more but is silent like Okie—

Later I go into my livingroom after a long sleep and my mother is sitting there with the furniture rearranged and some of it missing, bare, dark, sad, I say 'What are you doing?'—she is brooding, alone, sits in the middle of the triangle of chair and table with head lowered in long widow's despair—she whose face last night I saw bending over my sleep with an expression of unfathomable meaning I know is love on earth—and who was ironing all my clothes while I had these tragic dreams—

5

Big flaming airplanes trying to land in the New York-New Jersey airport in broad daylight; disaster two of them are floundering across the sky to crash in the meadows of junk—I'm watching from the field after a bus trip from somewhere North where I had a suitcase and a bag of big marbles (big bag) and stored them in the bus compartment myself in an attempt to save the marbles (for Lil Luke) after I'd goofed and taken a walk down the bus hi-way city then I saw I had to get back as soon as possible and only way to be on time was cab, more expensive than the bus trip itself!—so hurried—and now in field the DC-6's falling in orange sweptback flame.

Later according to instructions contained in the Almanac of Mystery and mark't on the Map of Bayonne, I go to Bayonne to the Ottoman Temple older than America made of wood Byzantium in splintered grey cracks, so old, like the barges at Communipaw waters—I sneak around on dangerous boards looking for the altar, I can see all big glittering New York across the river—it ends up I'm inside naked with little Philip and someone else presumably my young sister and we're all naked. I'm trying to take my choice but at same time I'm concerned (because pale and infantile) with other things, like airplanes and meaning of Temples—It was an Arabic Pseudomorphic overlay on the rusts of Jersey that no historian had yet noticed and it was so strange, it has to do with those knives and Burma caves of horror, something's deep inside, rituals of Snake and Old Sanskrit Secrets—Who was That He Man who wanted to fight me? I sure was ready for him.

6

That recurrent dream where I'm always in California in Frisco, and have to travel all the way back and have no money—I see a woman suspended in midair giving her son a strange rich pie thru a window of a wooden Frisco building, which he accepts graciously over the rushing traffics of the street, and I think first of Evelyn (Pomeray) in Los Gatos and the sad trains there-to, then I think of Ma in the East (N.Y.?) and how I gotta go home for Christmas.

There've been events all night, a bloody season, Irwin Gardens everywhere, Codies, et ceteras, I've had my up-to-here—it's time to go—wearing that seedy topcoat and my muffcap over my ears there I go driving down the spectral boulevard in an old car (it's actually Cody's '40 Packard) and I think of hitch hiking all in the snow and decide, 'Wyoming? No! I'll just drive all the way, at same time get this car home' (it's been given me)—What will I do for gas money? From hitch hikers—I'll work! 'But if I work I won't make it for Christmas!'—the whole spectral hump of the continent's ahead of me, ephemeral as now, awful as Edom— my Arcady of Ribs, my Troy of Bones I'll crack and Waterloo on such a hopeless run and as if not remarmant and cartchaptoed enuf and once again and *again again!*

But there I am already, driving wrong way on the Oneway boulevard and seeing I can't turnoff I make a neat proud U-turn and go back where I started from still debating how to make that 3,000 miles east, in that miserable coat and muff hat, driving slow like an old man, sunk low at the seat—'La Marde'—and all on account of a pie.

What an arbitrary conception this Coming Home For Christmas is—I've done it twice now, and each time it bugged out on me— the first time my mother fell asleep, the second time she had to go to a funeral—big gay cities have huge sad cemeteries right outside.

Rattling tenements and spectral girls (I call them tenements, I mean the wooden houses of San Fran—like the one Rosemarie jumped off-of), this drear dreaming of necessitous sad travelling and I wake up in a vast comfortable double bed in Rocky Mount in a house in the country with nothing to do but write Visions of Gerard, wash the dishes and feed the cat!—and pop the Book of Dreams—Can't remember the haunting, taunting earlier details of this dream, the girls, cops, floors, sex, suicides, pies, pastiches, parturiences, wallpapers, transcendencies—the stations grey Garden, who never laughs, mines information—June Ogilvie, Blabbery Adams McCracken, my girl—June John Boabus Prota-polapalopos, the Greek All-Mix Lover—Pain Twang—

7

The Flying horses of Mien Mo—I'm riding a bus thru Mexico with Cody sleeping at my side, at the dawn the bus stops in the countryside and I look out at the quiet warm fields and think: 'Is this really Mexico? Why am I here?'—The fields look too calm and grassy and bugless to be Mexico.

Later I'm sitting on the other side of the bus, Cody is gone, I look up in the sky and see that old ten thousand foot or hundred mile high mountain cliff with its enormous hazy blue palaces and temples where they have giant granite benches and tables for Giant Gods bigger than the ones who hugged skyscrapers on Wall Street.

And in the air, ah the silence of that horror, I see flying winged horses with capes furling over their shoulders, the slow majestic pawing of their front hooves as they clam thru the air flight—Griffins they are!—So I realise we're in 'Coyocan' and this is the famous legendary place—I start telling 4 Mexicans in the seat in front of me the story of the Mountain of Coyocan and its Secret Horses, but they laugh not only to hear a stranger talk about it but the ridiculousness of anybody even mentioning or noticing it— There's some secret they won't tell me concerning ignoration of the Frightful Castle—they even get wise with Gringo Me and I feel sand pouring down my shirt front, the big Mexican is sitting there with sand in his hand, smiling—I leap up and grab one, he is very tiny and skinny and I hold his hand against his belly so he won't pull a knife on me but he has none—They're really laughing at me for my big ideas about the Mountain—

We arrive at Coyocan town over which the hazy blue Mountain rises and now I notice that Flying Horses are constantly swirling over this town and around the cliff, swooping, flying, sometimes sweeping low, yet nobody looks and bothers with them. I can't bring myself to believe that they are actually flying horses and I look and look but that's what they have to be, even when I see them in moon profile: horses pawing thru air, slow, slow, eerie griffing horror men-horses—I realise they've been there all the time swirling around the Eternal Mountain Temple and I think: 'The bastards have something to do with that Temple, that's where they come from, I always knew that Mountain was all horror!'

I go inside the Coyocan Maritime Union Hall to sign for a Chinese sea job, it's in the middle of Mexico, I don't know why I've come all the way from New York to the landlocked centre of Mexico for a sea voyage, but there it is: a Seaman's hiring hall full of confusion and pale officials who don't understand why I came also—One of them makes a great intelligent effort to have letters in duplicate written to New York to begin a straightening out the reason why I came—So if it's a job I'll get, it won't be for a week at least, or *more*.

The town is evil and completely sinister because everybody is ugly sneering (the natives, I mean) and they refuse to recognise the existence of that Terrible Swirl of Flying Horses—'Mien Mo,' I think, remembering the name of the Mountain in Burma they call the world, with Dzapoudiba the southern island (India), on account of Himalayan secret horrors—The beating heart of the Giant Beast is up there, the Griffins are just incidental insects—but those Flying Horses are happy! How beautifully they claw slow fore-hooves thru the blue void!

Meanwhile 2 young American seamen and I study them flying up there miles high and watch them swoop lower, when they come low they change into blue and white birds to fool everybody—Even I say: 'Yep, they're not flying horses, they only seem to be, they're Birds!' but even as I say that I see a distinct horse motioning lyrically thru the moon with a cape furling from his infernal shoulders—

A broken-nosed ex boxer approaches me hinting that for 50 cents a job can be arranged on a ship—He is so sinister and intense I'm afraid to even give him 50 cents—Up comes a blonde with her fiancé announcing her forthcoming marriage, but she interrupts her speech every now and then to wail on my joint in front of everybody in the streets of Coyocan!

And the Flying Horses of Mien Mo are galloping with silent ease in the happy empty air way up there—Tinkle Tinkle go the streets of Coyocan as the sun falls, but up there is all silence and the Giant Gods are up. How can I describe it?

8

We all stand for a Group Photograph in the yard of the great Pine Tree Mansion of the Captors—later we play in the field, a hundred of us. I see Cody giving the rear man's hiball sign to a departing freight train and places a little Brakeman Doll in the tracks who also cranked-up tinily gives same sign as the train goes off to the outer world—We're all prisoners of the Communists.

Finally they ask us back for the group photo on the lawn leeringly saying 'Quite a few faces missing!' which I notice is true as I'm the last one to appear and the ranked standers are depleted—But they wave me away from the picture contemptuously down the dungeon steps. I've been suspected of revolutionary or at least bugged tendencies as I yakked in the 'Free Field'— Down I go to my doom—An insane attendant down the brown stone steps has me sit temporarily in a cell which has a large pool of brown water in a big pan with shit floating in it while I'm to be processed by him, but he leaves momentarily on a call so I rock the cell shiplike somehow and dump the brown shit water out into the dungeon aisle—But he gets back just as I'm doing it, picks up the pan and dumps it on my head and then on *his* head and we stare at each other dripping brown shit water hair and I realise among other things that the attendants of the Lower Hells are so miserably agonised they want you to be the same as they.

But meanwhile I understand that the Underground Prisons have women cooks and waitresses who need man-love so badly that they have developed a super secret subterranean system of their own to hie men away into sumptuous underground love-making apartments and the Authorities never know where they've vanished—the secret word is so secret and feminine they've tokens of admission to stud so mysterious; you can spend the rest of your captive life just boffing these luscious thin blondes completely secure and safe from harm—The 'tokens' are supposed to be 'food ration' buttons, but they're really what the women gather in work and pay to be allowed to visit the hidden captive men-places to be laid—And the Captor Authorities are forever puzzled—The insane attendant with shit water in his hair doesn't even know what's happened to you after you've been spirited away from his jurisdiction, not to mention the outside Firing-squad Photographers of the 'Free Yard'.

I AM DYING, MEESTER?

William Burroughs

While Cassady, Kerouac and others were searching for new experiences in America, several of their contemporaries were travelling much farther afield in the quest for self-awareness through drugs. And in this context there is no more important name than William S. Burroughs (1914–1997), one of the most authoritative literary voices on drugs and drug-addiction. He was, by his own admission, a heroin addict for fifteen years, having used not only heroin and its derivatives, but also other drugs in all their many forms, as comestibles, liquid, 'joints', or through injection. At the worst point of his heroin addiction he was injecting forty grains a day, and only by a supreme effort of will was he able to summon the courage to undergo treatment which eventually brought the habit under control. From his unique standpoint, he became a dedicated researcher and objective reporter into drugs of all kinds and contributed to both popular and scientific publications.

Burroughs' early life was one of intense study, particularly in the area of anthropology, but it was not until he moved to Europe that his real experimentation with drugs began. In subsequent years he became a 'walking pharmacy', to use his own words, trying narcotic, psychedelic and other drugs and travelling still farther afield to Central and South America and finally North Africa where the state of his addiction to heroin was finally brought home to him in Tangier. 'I lived in one room in the native quarter,' he later recalled. 'I had not taken a bath in a year nor changed my clothes . . . I did absolutely nothing. I could look at the end of my shoe for eight hours. I was only roused to action when the hourglass of junk ran out.' He finally found release from this horror in England and thereafter devoted himself to clearing up the misconceptions about the use of some drugs—and the potentialities of others.

William Burroughs' first book was the pseudonymous Junkie, *an account of his early addiction, published in 1953, which he concluded by stating that the telepathic-hallucinogenic-mind-expanding drug yage 'may be the final fix'. Found in the Amazon and used by tribal doctors, this drug so fascinated Burroughs that he travelled there especially to find it. He recorded his experiences in a series of letters to a then-unknown New York poet, Allen Ginsberg, and later the two men published their correspondence as* The Yage Letters *(1963). In these letters were also the 'first seeds' of the book which was to become* The Naked Lunch *(1959), Burroughs' masterly and famous evocation of his addiction. (The title, incidentally, was suggested to him by his old friend Jack Kerouac who referred to him as 'the last of the Faustian men'.) Later works evolved into surrealist satires such as* The Ticket that Exploded *and* Nova Express, *and Burroughs admitted that he frequently used cannabis while writing them as it 'activated trains of association that would otherwise be inaccessible'. He also wrote enthusiastically of mescaline— 'under its influence I have had the experience of fully seeing a painting for the first time'—but constantly warned of the 'treacherous and unpredictable nature of so many drugs'.*

Although he had his work occasionally banned and often viciously attacked, Burroughs became a champion of drug-inspired literature, but believed that 'the successful use of the experience depends on the skill of the writer'. In 1983 he was elected a member of the American Academy of Arts and Letters, and following his death at the age of 83 he was described in several obituaries as 'an icon of the Beat Generation'.

Surprisingly, selecting a short piece to represent him has proved one of the hardest tasks in compiling this book. In the end I have settled for this typical short story which is a result of his enquiries into yage and is one of his earliest experiments with the 'cut-up' technique which he helped to evolve. Here, then, is Burroughs the investigator of drugs, the explorer of the mind, and the adventurer into the farther realms of creative literature.

*   *   *

My work and understanding benefits from Hallucinogens measurably. Wider use of these drugs would lead to better work conditions on all levels.

Letter to Timothy Leary, 1970

Panama clung to our bodies—probably cut—Anything made this dream—It has consumed the customers of fossil orgasm—Ran into my old friend Jones—So badly off, forgotten, coughing in 1920 movie—Vaudeville voices hustle sick dawn breath on bed service—Idiot Mambo spattered backwards—I nearly suffocated trying on the boy's breath—That's Panama—Nitrous flesh swept out by your voice and end of receiving set—Brain eating birds patrol the low frequency brain waves—Post card waiting forgotten civilians 'and they are all on jelly fish, Meester—Panama photo town—Dead post card of junk.'

Sad hand down backward time track—Genital pawn ticket peeled his stale underwear—Brief boy on screen laughing my skivies all the way down—Whispers of dark street in Puerto Assis—Meester smiles through the village wastrel—Orgasm siphoned back telegram: 'Johnny pants down.'—(That stale summer dawn smell in the garage—Vines twisting through steel—Bare feet in dog's excrement.)

Panama clung to our bodies from Las Palmas to David on camphor sweet smells of cooking paregoric—Burned down the republic—The druggist no glot clom Fliday—Panama mirrors of 1910 under seal in any drug store—He threw in the towel, morning light on cold coffee—

Junk kept nagging me: 'Lushed in East St Louis, I knew you'd come scraping bone—Once a junky always spongy and rotten—I knew your life—Junk sick four days there.'

Stale breakfast table—little cat smile—Pain and death smell of his sickness in the room with me—Three souvenir shots of Panama city—Old friend came and stayed all day—Face eaten by 'I need more'—I have noticed this in the New World—'You come with me, Meester?'

And Joselito moved in at Las Playas during the essentials—Stuck in this place—Iridescent lagoons, swamp delta, gas flares—Bubbles of coal gas still be saying 'A ver, Luckees!' a hundred years from now—A rotting teak wood balcony propped up by Ecuador.

'The brujo began crooning a special case—It was like going under ether into the eyes of a shrunken head—Numb, covered with layers of cotton—Don't know if you got my last hints trying to break out of this numb dizziness with Chinese characters—All I want is out of here—Hurry up please—Took possession of me—How many plots have made a botanical expedition like this before they could take place?—Scenic railways—I am dying cross wine dizziness—I was saying over and over "shifted commissions where the awning flaps" Flashes in front of my eyes your voice and end of the line.'

That whinning Panama clung to our bodies—I went into Chico's Bar on mouldy pawn ticket, waiting in 1920 movie for a rum coke—Nitrous flesh under this honky tonk swept out by your voice: 'Driving Nails In My Coffin'—Brain eating birds patrol 'Your Cheating Heart'—Dead post card waiting a place forgotten—Light concussion of 1920 movie—Casual adolescent had undergone special GI processing—Evening on the boy's flesh naked—Kept trying to touch in sleep—'Old photographer trick wait for Johnny—Here goes Mexican cemetery.' On the sea wall met a boy with red and white striped T shirt—PG town in the purple twilight—The boy peeled off his stale underwear scraping erection—Warm rain on the iron roof—Under the ceiling fan stood naked on bed service—Bodies touched electric film, contact sparks tingled—Fan whiffs of young hard on washing adolescent T shirt—The blood smells drowned voices and end of the line—That's Panama—Sad movie drifting in islands of rubbish, black lagoons and fish people waiting a place forgotten—Fossil honky tonk swept out by a ceiling fan—Old photographer trick tuned them out.

'I am dying, Meester?'

Flashes in front of my eyes naked and sullen—Rotten dawn wind in sleep—Death rot on Panama photo where the awning flaps.

THE GREAT BEING

Allen Ginsberg

Several years after William Burroughs had completed his drug odyssey across half the world, an unknown poet with whom he had corresponded throughout his travels was to follow in his footsteps. He was Allen Ginsberg (1926–1997), now remembered as a major poet, a revolutionary-mystic figure and fêted as the leader of the 'amalgamated hippy-pacifist-activist-visionary-orgiastic-anarchist-Orientalist-psychedelic underground', to quote The New Yorker.

The son of a poet, Ginsberg was interested in writing from his youth and began experimenting with prose while at Columbia University, in the company of Jack Kerouac and others. He also began to experiment with drugs and sexual freedom and was eventually expelled by the authorities. After a period of moving from one job to another, he finally became a market researcher in San Francisco. Tiring of this job, too, he fell in again with Jack Kerouac and soon became a major influence in the development of the Beat Generation. His national and international reputation as a poet—not to mention the origins of the furore that constantly surrounded him—was made in 1956 when his first collection of poems, Howl, *was published by Lawrence Ferlinghetti who was subsequently prosecuted (unsuccessfully, as it turned out). This work, and those that followed, including the elegy* Kaddish, *openly revealed his homosexuality, his visionary mind and his passionate belief in the expansion of consciousness through the use of drugs, Hinduism and Zen Buddhism. In describing his own use of drugs, he said that he found peyote, marijuana, mescaline, ether and lysergic acid 'open up an aware-*

ness of the supernatural, of the godhead, and free the soul'. LSD, however, became the drug with which he was most closely identified and several of his poems—notably 'LSD 25' and 'Wales Visitation'—were actually written under its influence.

For much of the latter period of his life Ginsberg, who is credited with having coined the phrase 'flower power', lived in New York's East Village where he was regularly embroiled in controversy over his naked poetry readings, championing of radical causes and his encouragement of experimental writing. In all he published about forty collections of poems which 'liberated American poetry in the way that Look Back in Anger *revitalised British theatre', to quote* The Times, *and won the National Book Award for* The Fall of America *in 1972. The* 'enfant terrible *of the Beat Generation' (New York Times) also collaborated on songs with a number of leading contemporary musicians, including Bob Dylan, The Clash and Bono of U2. 'I venerated Kerouac and the others,' he once declared, 'to me they seemed like sacramental personages.'*

It was during some of his early travels in India and North Africa that Ginsberg began replying to the letters he had received nearly ten years earlier from William Burroughs. In this correspondence he described his own visions under the drug yage which had so enraptured Burroughs. One of these 'reports' is reprinted below, for not only does it fulfil the requirements of this collection in that it is full of visionary experience, but it also has much of the poetic construction and brilliant use of words that typify Ginsberg at the height of his powers.

*   *   *

On a trip, you enter corridors inside, and into the heart. Naturally, you'll come upon old feelings you didn't know were there and were ashamed of.

Interview in *Evergreen Review, 1969*

Went back and talked to The Maestro, gave him 35 soles ($1.50) for services and talked with him about peyote and LSD—he'd heard of peyote—he's a mestizo who studied in San Martin

(upper Huallaga territory)—he gave me samples of his mix—
uses young cultivated Ayahuasca plant in his back yard, and
mixes that about half and half with a catalyst known as the
'Mescla' which is another leaf known in Chama Indian language
as Cahua (pron Coura) and locally by him in Pucallpa is called
Chacruna. Said he'd get me more samples to bring back to Lima
Natural History Museum to identify. Cooks the mixes together
all day and strains the broth, gives the drained leaves a second
cook too. Anyway the preparation is not excessively secret—I
think Schultes saw and knows the preparation. Can add other
leaves of other plants, too, I don't know these combinations to
try out—he seemed generally interested in drugs—serious—and
not mercenary at all—good type—has quite a following here—
does physical cures, his speciality.

Anyway to make long story short, went back to formal group
session in huts last night—this time the brew was prepared fresh
and presented with full ceremony—he crooning (and blowing
cigarette or pipe smoke) tenderly over the cupmouth for several
minutes before—(enamel cup, I remember your plastic cup)—
then I light cigarette, blow a puff of smoke over cup, and drain.
Saw a shooting star—Aerolith—before going in, and full moon,
and he served me up first—then lay down expecting God knows
what other pleasant vision and then I began to get high—and
then the whole fucking cosmos broke loose around me, I think
the strongest and worst I've ever had it nearly—(I still reserve
the Harlem experiences, being Natural, in abeyance. The LSD
was Perfection but didn't get me so deep in nor so horribly
in)—First I began to realise my worry about the mosquitoes or
vomiting was silly as there was the great stake of life and Death—
I felt faced by Death, my skull in my beard on pallet on porch
rolling back and forth and settling finally as if in reproduction
of the last physical move I make before settling into real death—
got nauseous, rushed out and began vomiting, all covered with
snakes, like a Snake Seraph, coloured serpents in aureole all
around my body, I felt like a snake vomiting out the universe—
or a Jivaro in head-dress with fangs vomiting up in realisation
of the Murder of the Universe—my death to come—everyone's

death to come—all unready—I unready—all around me in the
trees the noise of these spectral animals the other drinkers vomiting (normal part of the Cure sessions) in the night in their awful
solitude in the universe—vomiting up their will to live, be pre-
served in this body, almost—Went back and lay down—Ramon
came over quite tender and nurse like (he hadn't drunk, he's sort
of an aide to help the sufferers) asked me if I was OK and 'Bien
Mareado' (Good and drunk?)—I said 'Bastante' and went back
to listen to the spectre that was approaching my mind—The
whole hut seemed rayed with spectral presences all suffering
transfiguration with contact with a single mysterious Thing that
was our fate and was sooner or later going to kill us—The
Curandero crooning, keeping up a very tender, repeated and then
changing simple tune, comfort sort of, God knows what signi-
fied—seemed to signify some point of reference I was unable to
contact yet—I was frightened and simply lay there with wave
after wave of death-fear, fright, rolling over me till I could hardly
stand it, didn't want to take refuge in rejecting it as illusion, for
it was too real and too familiar—especially as if in rehearsal of
Last Minute Death my head rolling back and forth on the blanket
and finally settling in last position of stillness and hopeless resignation of God knows what Fate—for my being—felt completely
lost strayed soul—outside of contact with some Thing that
seemed present—finally had a sense that I might face the Question there and then, and choose to die and understand—and leave
my body to be found in the morning—I guess grieving everybody—couldn't bear to leave Peter and my father so alone—
afraid to die yet then and so never took the Chance (if there was
a Chance, perhaps somehow there was)—also as if everybody
in session in central radiotelepathic contact with the same problem—the Great Being within ourselves—Coming back from
vomit saw a man knees to chest I thought I saw as X ray his
skull I realised he was crouched there as in a shroud (with towel
mosquito protection wrapped round his face) suffering the same
trial and separation—Thought of people, saw their images
clearly, you—mysterious apparently know more than I do now
and why don't you communicate, or can't you, or have I ignored

it?—Simon seemingly an angel in his annihilation of vanity and
giving forth new life in children—'If any interplanetary news
comes through' he said 'I'll be the first to be relaying it over the
wires in a way that won't get it fucked up'—Francine his wife—
sort of a Seraph of Woman, all women (as all men) the same—
spectral creatures put here mysteriously to live, be the living
Gods, and suffer Crucifixion of death like Christ, but either get
lost and die in soul or get in Contact and give new birth to
continue the Process of Being (tho' they themselves die, or do
they?)—and I lost and poor Peter who depends on me for some
Heaven I haven't got, lost—and I keep rejecting women, who
come to minister to me—decided to have children somehow, a
revolution in the Hallucination—but the suffering was about as
much as I could bear and the thought of more suffering even
deeper to come made me despair—felt, still feel, like lost soul,
surrounded by ministering angels (Ramon, the Maestro, yourself,
the whole Common World of Diers)—and my poor mother died
in God knows what state of suffering—I can't stand it—vomited
again (Ramon had come over and told me to vomit off the porch
where I was lying, if I had to later, very careful kind situation)
I mean, is this a good group—I remember your saying watch
out *whose* vision you get—but God knows I don't know who to
turn to finally when the Chips are down spiritually and I have to
depend on my own Serpent-self's memory of Merry Visions of
Blake—or depend on nothing and enter anew—but enter
what?—Death?—and at that moment—vomiting still feeling like
a Great lost Serpent-seraph vomiting in consciousness of the
Transfiguration to come—with the Radiotelepathy sense of a
Being whose presence I had not yet fully sensed—too Horrible
for me, still—to accept the fact of total communication with say
everyone an eternal seraph male and female at once—and me a
lost soul seeking help—well slowly the intensity began to fade,
I being incapable of moving in any direction spiritually—not
knowing who to look to or what to look for—not quite trusting
to ask the Maestro—tho' in the vision of the scene it was he
who was the local logical Ministering Spirit to trust, if anyone—
went over and sat by him (as Ramon gently suggested) to be

The Vomiter

'blown'—that is he croons a song to you to cure your soul and blows smoke at you—rather a comforting presence—tho' by now the steep fear had passed—that being over got up and took my piece of cloth I brought against mosquitoes and went home in moonlight with plump Ramon—who said the more you saturate yourself with Ayahuasca the deeper you go—visit the moon, see the dead, see God—see Tree Spirits—etc.

I hardly have the nerve to go back, afraid of some real madness, a Changed Universe permanently changed—tho' I guess change it must for me someday—much less as planned before, go up the river six hours to drink with an Indian tribe—I suppose I will—meanwhile will wait here another week in Pucallpa and drink a few more times with the same group—I wish I knew who, if anyone, there is to work with that *knows*, if anyone knows, who I am or what I am. I wish I could hear from you. I think I'll be here long enough for a letter to reach me—write.

THE AMERICAN EXPRESS

Gregory Corso

According to Seymour Krim in his study The Beats *(1960),
Gregory Corso (1930–   ) is 'one of the big beat three that began
to turn the public on around 1954; Kerouac and Ginsberg the
other two.' Described at the time as urchin-looking, street-bred
and a loving wordsman with lots of humour, it is also said of
him that if Kerouac was the father-figure of the movement and
Ginsberg the rabbi-figure, he was the child-figure and the clown.
But Corso, perhaps even more than the others, was the most
ardent apologist of the Beats, promoting the anti-social, apoca-
lyptic, love-centred, freedom-loving mystique they all shared and
which soon became so familiar to the world. His verse collections
like* Gasoline *and* Bomb, *both published by City Lights in 1958,
quickly established his reputation: the poem 'Bomb', printed in
the shape of a mushroom cloud, showed a richness of invention
and an obsession with death which are two of his recognised
hallmarks.*

*Born into a poor immigrant family in Manhattan, Corso had
a tough childhood and was a juvenile delinquent when barely
into his teens. By the time he was 20 he had spent three years
in prison for robbery. But it was here that he began to read
avidly and after his release set about self-educating himself. In
1955 his first collection of poems,* The Vestal Lady of Brattle,
was published, and also a play, The Hung-Up Age, *and as a
result of these he was 'discovered' by Kerouac and Ginsberg
who saw him as one of their own. Kerouac became a strong
influence on Corso's subsequent work—and life-style—which
earned him the reputation of being the perennial bad boy, hipster*

and rebel, and saw him mixing powerful statements with bombast in his poems. Travel in Europe and India broadened his work and stimulated his interest in drugs which he expressed in collections such as The Happy Birthday of Death *(1960)—a title he chose after toying with 'The Rumpled Backyard', 'Fried Shoes', 'Radiator Soup' and 'Gargoyle Liver'—and* Elegiac Feelings American *(1970), dedicated to 'the dear memory of John Kerouac' and used as an attack on America for its destruction of Kerouac. His journeys also inspired his only novel,* The American Express, *published in Paris in 1961, from which the following hallucinatory episode is taken. During the Seventies Corso began to lead a more settled life as a member of the Department of English at the State University of New York at Buffalo where he taught and continued writing poetry. Subsequently he has moved to California where he now lives in remote obscurity.*

* * *

I am a mental explorer, un-Faustian
My verse is hopeful—naïve—strange—sweet—soon smart—why not.
Elegiac Feelings American, 1970

Joel had entered a war that was new and shining. A war that was an adventure.

And the fighting was to be a youthful heroic game to be played with exuberance and joy, without fear.

The old soldier could not understand Joel's zest. 'Woe,' he would say, 'woe to the sinful nation, to a people laden with iniquity!'

'History, life! has been made rich! by war,' sang Joel.

The old man grabbed him by the collar. 'The armies of a people scattered and peeled, and a nation meted out and trodden down—'

Captain Blaze rode up to the two men. 'Joel! Go to the battlefield and tell General Eatsun Smacknight's men are sacking and looting the town—tell him we need reinforcements! Hurry, make haste!'

'Yes sir!' And Joel jumped on his horse and was off.

At the start of the battle between the two armies led by Eatsun and Smacknight thousands of men wearing bright colourful uniforms stood facing each other at a distance of an encompassed smooth green field. The sun shone on the scene as though it were watching nothing else in all the world. The two armies were perfectly aligned, levied, flanked, and prepared to fight. They were men made for the occasion. They had no other thought or purpose but to charge, enter, clash, and overcome the enemy.

The two generals faced each other with their vast armies. They raised their arms; the lowering of them would signal the start of the onslaught.

Joel thundered urgency on a magnificent black horse. He reached the battlefield and brought his horse to a screaming halt before General Eatsun. 'Sir! The enemy is spreading disorder and terror in town—they are sacking and looting, women and children are being slaughtered—'

'The battle will prove decisive here!' roared the general.

'But Captain Blaze said they will move north—they will come from behind—'

'You tell Captain Blaze to evacuate!'

'Yes sir!' And Joel pulled the reins of his horse, the horse stood up and turned in a wonderfully graceful fashion, and Joel was off.

The signalling arms went down, the onslaught was on.

Five of Smacknight's men were in hot pursuit of Joel.

Along the embankment of the river sat Thimble and Mr D with binoculars, watching all.

The horsemen of both sides charged across the field like a rising music, and behind them the footmen screamed animal cries as they ran sword-arms raised and swinging, and the banner carriers at the lead raced into each other and in immediate succession the entire horde interlocked into a riotous knot of death—heads fell, hands fell, hearts were pierced, necks were broken, axe rang

on axe and sword resounded on sword—the swiftness, and the
fierceness, helmet-tumblings, and horses neighing, falling—knit
upon knit until the whole violently chaotic spool was so hideously
strange that it affected Nature to such an extent that all the trees
in the vicinity went insane.

The five horsemen were catching up with Joel. He was not too
far away from the besieged town—he held the neck of his horse
and galloped mercilessly, occasionally turning to see the progress
of his pursuers.

The townspeople were evacuating. The manager of the American Express and staff packed everything they could possibly carry
and left. Hinderov immediately came out of the basement with
a bucket of black paint and a brush.

'Victory!' he cried as he crossed out the AMERICAN from the
windows and put, in its place, HINDEROV. And so it was that
the American Express became the Hinderov Express. Bronskier
jumped with joy—'Hinderov, you've won! It's all yours!' And,
fate of fates, a bullet of war touched Bronskier's face—Albie
hurried in horror to his father's side—Bronskier was dead.

Albie held his father in his arms. 'Hear! O Great Queen of
arms, whose favour my father won, as you defend the sire, defend

the son. When on Hinderov's cause the banded powers of war he left, and sought the American Express, peace was his charge; received with peaceful show, he went a legate, but returned a foe—' Albie rose and walked towards Hinderov with murder in his eyes. Hinderov backed away. 'What's wrong with you? Are you crazy? What are you doing—' and Hinderov backed away, and Albie came on.

'You fool! You dare to threaten me!' croaked Hinderov.

'You are the enemy of man, Hinderov—'

At that moment a sergeant rode up to them. 'What regiment do you guys belong to?'

Hinderov sighed relief. 'I know nothing about army arrangements, sergeant, but I would like to join a regiment—'

'Go east,' ordered the sergeant, 'the operations of our troops there have caused the enemy to break through—they are occupying positions within the territories of our land! Have you a horse?'

'No, sir—'

Albie stood sadly by the body of his father; he would have to bury him.

'And you!' called the sergeant; 'have you any orders?'

'No—'

'What are you doing?'

'I will bury my father–'

Joel reached Captain Blaze and told him what General Eatsun had ordered.

'Damned Eatsun!' cursed the wearied, battle-worn captain; 'he's ever bringing fresh orders, has he any idea where his military garrisons are held up? It's a queer business—nothing seems to come from the regimental staff; what are these telephones for? Not once have they called—what kind of staff is it that doesn't telephone its orders to the battalion? I did not have to adhere to Eatsun's orders, dammit!'

Joel, exhausted by his mission, sat down by the old soldier. The old soldier smiled and handed Joel a cup of coffee. Surrounding them were burning houses, and dying men, and dead men, and screaming women, and crying babies—

'It's hell—' said Joel.

The old soldier shook a finger at Joel. 'So long as a man is in this world he is midway between hell and heaven; hell is yet to be seen, m'boy—'

A wounded soldier grappling his shot stomach fell in terrible agony before Joel.

'But this is not what I thought it would be!' cried Joel, dropping his cup of coffee.

'Watch him,' said the old soldier, 'watch the carbon leave him. It's carbon that separates the living from the dead—it'll soon leave him—watch—'

'The poor man!'

'The thing about carbon,' continued the old man, 'is that it makes a basis for life in its ability to form, with other chemicals, extremely complex molecules—'

The dying soldier raised a death-reaching hand into life for help . . . Joel knelt beside him and rested the poor man's head on his lap. Joel wished he were on his horse, moving fast. Everything seemed alive and exciting when he moved. Suddenly a machine-gun assault mowed down Captain Blaze and the group of strategists surrounding him. The machine-gun unit fired for almost an hour on the trapped regiment. After the bloody engagement, Captain Blaze's men, who were decisively outnumbered, fled in confusion and panic.

Josl jumped up and raced to his horse.

'Take me!' cried the old soldier, 'I haven't a horse—please take me!'

'Hurry!'

And the old soldier with desperate agility climbed on the horse—and Joel, with bullets whizzing all about, thundered off, the old soldier embracing his small waist.

Joel returned to the battlefield. Night was falling. In the sky crows dipped and climbed—the battle was over.

Generals Eatsun and Smacknight and their armies lay where they had fallen.

'The cords of death compassed me about, the cords of hell encompassed me, the snares of death forestalled me: therefore

He sent out His arrows, and many lightnings, and discomfited them. I will pursue mine enemies, and catch them, neither will I turn until I have consumed them. I will smite them that they shall not be able to rise. Thou hath girded me with strength unto this war, and Thou shalt put mine enemies to flight; I will beat them small as dust before the faces of the wind, as the mire of the streets I will enfeeble them—'

Mr D and Thimble were captured by the enemy. They were simply walking along the highway expounding theories about the battle that they had earlier witnessed when a band of Smack-night's soldiers engulfed them. They were brought to the enemy camp, and there they were both tied to a pole in a big tent.

'Well, lord love a duck, are they going to shoot us or eat us—' wondered Thimble.

Mr D made a wry face as he tried to ease the tightness of the rope around his wrists—'Stupid birdbrains! Don't even know how to tie a man up!'

'Smacknight definitely lost that encounter today,' stated Thimble. They both sat back to back with the pole in between.

'Seems like they're winning as far as we're concerned. How we gonna get out of here!'

'Here comes someone now—'

It was a big black-haired man dressed in jangling armour, followed by four soldiers.

The soldiers put a little stool before the two tied men, and the big man sat on it, smiling, his teeth gleaming, his long black moustache cringing—and he rested his fat hands on his widened knees and leaned into Mr D and Thimble—'Dogs! Swine! Spies!'

The two men said nothing.

'Do you deny you are spies!'

'We were taking a stroll,' said Thimble.

'You were spying!'

'Can you loosen these ropes somewhat,' asked Mr D, still preoccupied with the bungled binding.

'Shut up!' the big man shouted. 'I'll do the talking! Dogs! Lice! You are both guilty of spying; the penalty for spying is death. You will both be shot immediately!' And the big man jangling with silver and swords strutted out of the tent.

'Well, D, this looks like it—'

The four soldiers gathered about them and cut them free.

'Not so, Thimble! They're not going to get Mr D!' And Mr D, a tall thin humble-looking man, transformed into a fury of a man. He swung at the soldier closest to him with all his might and the soldier fell back into the other three. Thimble quickly picked up the stool and swung it blindly in all directions, and it connected with two soldiers. The other two soldiers drew their swords but Mr D was on top of them with a heavy plank of wood and he brought it down upon their helmeted heads—it was done rapidly, in a matter of seconds, and the four soldiers lay still at their feet.

Mr D picked up a sword and slashed the back of the tent. He and Thimble hurried out. It was night, and they ran like the wind into it.

After they were in the clear Thimble suggested they inform Eatsun's forces of the enemy's position but Mr D advised against it, stating that both forces were obviously implements of death, and so meant them no good.

Joel assumed command of the army. He sat breathlessly before the battlefield. The battle had ceased but would shortly be resumed.

BOOM!

Joel raced into the muddy attack swinging swords and knives, shooting rifles and stens, flinging grenades and flares; and everybody dispersed in his path, and he skipped through the dispersion like a happy girl.

Tanks loomed before him; he threw tankbomb after tankbomb, and the tanks became all afire—

He shot the burning men teeming out of the burning tanks like a hard cold man.

The battle was over; he walked over the dead like an old market woman.

WHERE IS VIETNAM?

Lawrence Ferlinghetti

As the patron and publisher of a number of the writers included in this book, Lawrence Ferlinghetti (1920–   ) believed with Walt Whitman that the duty of the poet is to be an agitator. He became one of the founders and chief impresario of the Beats, sharing Jack Kerouac's credo that 'Beat is the soul of beatific', and early in his career experimented with writing poetry while under the influence of LSD. Ferlinghetti said he took the substance not out of hedonism, but instead—in the words of the title of one of his collections—to find The Secret Meanings of Things *(1969). He developed an experimental technique of writing which owed much to e.e. cummings, and his language was often shocking. In all his work, Ferlinghetti celebrates love, sex and freedom while attacking crass materialism in equal measure.* A Coney Island of the Mind, *which he published in 1958, was for years one of the all-time best-selling collections of poetry.*

Although he was born in New York, Ferlinghetti lived in France with his family for four years during the early 1920s. Thereafter he returned to America to study at the Bronxville Public School and at the University of North Carolina where he took a BA in journalism. During the Second World War he served in the United States Naval Reserve before finally settling in San Francisco in 1951, where he taught French. Alert to the emergence of a new wave of writers, he founded the City Lights Bookshop two years later. Many of the books he has published reflect his own interests and concerns, but despite the impressive roster of his discoveries he admits to having mistakenly turned down William Burroughs' The Naked Lunch *because he thought it was 'too much a junkie's vision of hell' and regrets not having been able to persuade Henry Miller, a friend, to join his list. 'I always admired Miller's gusto,' he explains, 'but I think he was kind of jealous of the writers we had, and he didn't want to be associated with Ginsberg and company. These guys were stealing his sexual thunder.'*

Since the 1960s, while most of the other Beats have died or drifted away from the literary world, Lawrence Ferlinghetti has remained a powerful force with no sign of watering down his ideals. He continues to publish and encourage young writers who share his belief that artists should be 'gadflies, yea-sayers to humanity, nay-sayers to the forces of repression'. In 1988 he published his second novel, Love in the Days of Rage *(the first,* Her, *had been written 28 years earlier), which he describes as 'ecstatic fiction—meaning prose that builds up to some kind of ecstatic climax'.*

Ferlinghetti particularly hated the Vietnam war, and the following item, written in July 1965, neatly rounds off this part of the book with its unique slant on one of the consuming obsessions of Sixties writers.

*   *   *

I think it's the duty of the artist to be subversive—just by definition of being the bearer of eros, the love-seeking, light-seeking being, the poet is the enemy of the state.

Starting from San Francisco, 1961

Meanwhile back at the Ranch the then President also known as Colonel Cornpone got out a blank army draft and began to fill in the spaces with men and Colonel Cornpone got down to the bottom of the order where there is a space to fill in to indicate just where the troops are to be sent and Colonel Cornpone got a faraway look in his eye and reached out and started spinning a globe of the world that lay ready at hand to be spun and Colonel Cornpone looked at the spinning globe with that faraway look and his eye wandered over the spinning surface of the world and after a long time he said I See No Relief! so they brought him a relief map of the world and he looked at it a long time and

said Thank you gentlemen I see it all clearly now yes everything
stands out very clearly now I can see the oceans themselves
rolling back and Western civilisation really is still marching
Westward around the world and the New Frontier now truly
knows no boundaries anywhere and those there Vietnamese don't
stand a Chinaman's chance in hell but still there's all those
Chinamen think they do and think they can actually reverse this
here Westward march of civilisation and reverse the natural Westward spinning of this here globe and I have a report here General
which reports that quote 'The machine-gunner was shooting them
down as fast as he could but there were just more people coming
at him than there were bullets coming out of his machine-gun'
said Sgt George A. Vanlandingham of Alexandria Va. describing
the assault in which our military Advisers were somehow caught
in the backfire of their own Advice unquote and Colonel
Cornpone got that old faraway look again and said Gentlemen
these are not wargames this is not Space Angels this is the real
thing gentlemen and you and I know exactly where this here
Vietnam is General but maybe some of the press here and some
of our own people may not know right exactly where this here
Vietnam is gentlemen and I want you all to make very sure that
you do in case anybody gets cornered by some eggheads or
somebody And just then Ladybird came running and Colonel
Cornpone stepped into a cloakroom and whispered to her Just
where is that there Hanoi? and she being smarter than he as is
usually the case whispered back that this here Vietnam was not
a place at all but a state of mind And Colonel Cornpone got that
faraway look again and stepped back onto the front porch of his
Ranch where they keep the rockers and he sat there rocking for
a long time and then he said Gentlemen I am a family man and
this is for real and I am now ordering the complete and final
liberation of Vietmind I mean Vietnam for the roots of the trouble
are found wherever the landless and despised the poor and
oppressed stand before the gates of opportunity and are not
allowed across the Frontier into the Great Society and so gentlemen here we go fasten your seatbelts we are powerful and free
and we have a destiny and so gentlemen let me point out to you

all exactly where it is we are going on this here globe because even though I have never been out of the United States of America I know just exactly where we're going on the brink of Vietmind I mean Vietnam and even though we don't want to stop the world spinning in the right direction even for a moment I want to slow it down just long enough for all of us to get our bearings so that I may put my finger for you exactly on this here sore spot which is Vietmine I mean Vietnam And Colonel Cornpone put out his hand to slow down the world just a bit but this world would not be stopped this world would not stop spinning at all and Texas and Vietnam spun on together faster and faster slipping away faster and faster under Colonel Cornpone's hand because the surface of this world had suddenly become very slippery with a strange kind of red liquid that ran on it across all the obscene boundaries and this world went on spinning faster and faster in the same so predestined direction and kept on spinning and spinning and spinning and spinning!

2

I think that any value has been to help create the next step. I don't think there will be any movement on the drug scene until there is something else to move to.

KEN KESEY (1935–)
in *The Electric Kool-Aid Acid Test* (1968) by Tom Wolfe

In April 1943, while the rest of Europe was engaged in war, a scientist in neutral Switzerland was working for the Sandoz drug company on research into the ergot fungus that affects rye. On 16 April, Albert Hofmann accidentally ingested a minute quantity of the substance he was studying. He had taken the first-ever 'acid trip'. Hofmann had discovered LSD.

The new drug caused something of a stir among forward-looking psychologists. Many of the experiences described and symptoms exhibited by those who took LSD resembled those of patients diagnosed as schizophrenic. A few of these psychologists—Doctors Timothy Leary and Richard Alpert among them—realised the importance of Hofmann's discovery: that LSD was the most powerful, and potentially easily available, consciousness-changing substance known to man; and more important, they had some inkling of the effect that this discovery would have in a wider sphere.

The Veterans' Hospital at Menlo Park in California was engaged in 1959 on a programme involving LSD. Their 'guinea-pigs' were paid $75 per session. Among these guinea-pigs was a young novelist, Ken Kesey. Tom Wolfe, in *The Electric Kool-Aid Acid Test*, has described Kesey's feelings after taking LSD: 'The whole thing was . . . *the experience* . . . this certain indescribable *feeling* . . . Indescribable, because words can only jog the memory, and there is no memory of . . . The *experience* of the barrier between the subjective and objective, the personal and the impersonal, the *I* and the *not-I* disappearing . . . that feeling!' Kesey at once realised the potential of this new drug, and he knew how to get more.

Aldous Huxley had already described his experiences of taking mescaline in 1953 in his essays 'The Doors of Perception' and 'Heaven and Hell'. He had had an immense influence on many of those who were anxious to try mescaline, which was becoming more easily available, and LSD. Alan Watts took LSD in 1961 and wrote about his experiences in *The Joyous Cosmology*. Huxley's and Watts's approaches to the LSD experience were essentially similar. They were intellectuals with a particular interest in mysticism and they were in search of 'the deeper, or higher, levels of insight that can be reached through these consciousness-changing "drugs" when accompanied with sustained philosophical reflection by a person who is in search, not of kicks, but of understanding,' to use Watts's words. Their 'trip' would take place in a white room, with beautiful paintings and objects or scenery at hand, a piano concerto on the record-player, and they would there engage in 'sustained philosophical reflection'. It was an approach that, to begin with at least, was adopted by Leary and Alpert, who regarded LSD as a sacrament. The experience was something holy, and should, they recommended, be taken with an experienced 'guide' at hand.

Meanwhile Ken Kesey was assembling around him a group of people equally anxious to experiment with the new drugs—including, inevitably, Neal Cassady. They became known as the Merry Pranksters. The Pranksters are now a legend, but it is important to realise their place in the history of the new 'drug culture'. Essentially, the achievement of Kesey and the Pranksters was to free LSD from the doctors and the intellectuals. They would ingest indiscriminate amounts of LSD and rather than remaining quietly in a white room, they took to the roads in a multicoloured bus with FURTHER emblazoned on its front. What is more, they presented a series of 'acid tests', at which the audience, all supplied with LSD, would be bombarded by sound, light and any other phenomena that the collective mind of the Pranksters could produce. Nothing could be farther from the approach of Huxley or Watts. Others, of course, had made the same discovery independently of Kesey and his particular group. The word spread, and soon thousands of young people were taking LSD and the so-called psychedelic drugs, and from the viewpoint of the intellectuals and the mystics they were taking them for kicks.

However, each LSD trip contains within it the potentiality for both a religious experience and for 'kicks'; in the course of his trip, the voyager is likely to experience both. Much depends upon his set and setting. One thing *is* certain. Having taken LSD he will not view the world around him in quite the same way. As Robert Hunter has remarked in *The Storming of the Mind*, '[LSD] removes the individual from the context of his culture. It takes him—however temporarily—away from the familiar board, renders the normal rules of the game useless, and opens him up to a radically-altered perception.' In effect, turning on with LSD is a political act. In the early Sixties this was realised, at most, hazily. It was to take a few years for the full realisation to dawn. In the early days the important thing was that 'there was no tragedy in LSD and mescaline and pot as long as one was involved in a sincere search,' to quote Hank Harrison in *The Dead Book*. In short—as he went on still more succinctly—'After LSD everything was colour; prior to LSD everything was a cruddy, black-and-white schmaze.'

In November 1990, Ken Kesey, who since 1959 had written two novels, *One Flew Over the Cuckoo's Nest* (1962) and *Sometimes a Great Notion* (1964), neither dealing with drug-taking, created a sense of *déjà vu* for all those with fond memories of the Beat Generation by re-running his original bus trip in FURTHER to promote his memoirs of the Sixties, *The Further Inquiry*. The bus painted in day-glo colours was not the original 1939 International Harvester that had helped to give a new meaning to the concept of taking a trip. Nonetheless it caught the attention of the American public and the media alike, attracting, as the *New York Herald Tribune* described them, 'a load of balding hipsters fuelled not with LSD but an elixir of bourbon and Evian water', with Kesey joking to those who suspected the switch, 'Never trust a Prankster!'

LSD IS AIR

Timothy Leary

*Timothy Leary (1921–1996), was the most famous name connec-
ted with drugs and, according to* Playboy *magazine, the man
who 'was transmogrified from scientist and researcher into pro-
genitor and high priest of a revolutionary movement spawned
not by an idea but by a substance that's been called the "spiritual
equivalent of the hydrogen bomb".'*

*Leary came to his involvement with drugs as a middle-aged
man. Brought up as a Roman Catholic, he abandoned the Church
as a student, and then walked out of West Point military academy
before settling for a life of scholastic study and graduating as a
psychologist. In 1960 he was lecturing on clinical psychology at
Harvard when he underwent the experience that was to change
his entire life. He was on holiday at the time in Cuernacava in
Mexico, when he ate seven strange-looking mushrooms he had
bought from a local doctor and felt himself 'swept over the edge
of a sensory niagara into a maelstrom of transcendental visions
and hallucinations'. The fungi were the legendary Aztec sacred
mushrooms or 'Flesh of God', and Leary's experiences over the
ensuing five hours not only radically affected much of his thinking, but set him on the path to becoming the pioneer investigator
in an area of drug experience now much emulated throughout
the world. Returning to Harvard, Leary began to experiment
systematically with the chemical derivative of the mushroom,
psilocybin, and encouraged his colleagues and students to do the
same and thereby explore 'inner space'. As his following grew,
Leary experimented with other substances, including morning
glory seeds, peyote, nutmeg, mescaline and, finally, LSD, which*

he soon decided was the most exciting and powerful of them all. Word of these 'trips' quickly began to spread, and in 1963 Leary and his colleague Richard Alpert were dismissed from Harvard. He tried, unsuccessfully, to found a colony for drug research in Mexico, and was eventually sent back to America by the authorities. In 1966 he tried again to establish a centre for his work at Millbrook in New York state, but was harassed and finally raided by the police and charged with possession of marijuana. His subsequent fight against conviction, his ten-year sentence and imprisonment, escape to Africa in 1970 and deportation back to America, made him a messiah to his followers and a scourge of the establishment.

Leary published numerous articles on his work and several books, including the important High Priest *(1968) which propounded his philosophy and related it to the discoveries and writings of others. Of himself Leary said, 'At the time I had my first psychedelic experience, I was a 39-year-old man involved in the middle-aged process of dying. My joy in life, my sensual openness, my creativity, were all sliding downhill. Since that time my life has been renewed in almost every dimension.' A reporter who saw him 'on the run' in Algiers in 1971 found a different picture: 'He has now taken over 300 trips on psilocybin and LSD—averaging one a week. His hair is grey; his conversation has changed. Some people suggest he has suffered permanent brain damage . . .' Later, visitors to Leary in prison found him alert and filled with energy, however, and he had moved on, beyond drugs, in two further books* Terra II *and* Neurologic.

'Uncle Tim', as Leary became known among his followers, and 'the most dangerous man in the world', according to Richard Nixon, spent about 42 months of his life in 40 different prisons because of his beliefs. His involvement with LSD gained him many young admirers, as well as friendships with Aldous Huxley and William Burroughs, plus a life-long notoriety which he encouraged with headline-making stories. One of these claimed he rode around the grounds of his mansion at Millbrook, New York, on a horse painted blue on one side and pink on the other; while in 1969 he announced he was standing for the Governorship

of California, promising to abolish taxes and run the state as a business. In the closing years of his life, until his death from prostate cancer in Los Angeles in June 1996, he joined the lecture circuit, invented a number of video and computer games, and expressed an admiration for space migration. His dying wish was that an urn containing his ashes should be strapped to a rocket and sent into orbit.

The essay reprinted here represents the Timothy Leary of 1968.

*   *   *

I'm saying simply that sex under LSD becomes miraculously enhanced and intensified. It increases your sensitivity a thousand per cent. Merging, yielding, flowing, union, communion. It's all love-making; you're in pulsating harmony with all the energy around you.

Interview in *Playboy*, 1966

The loneliness of long nights in that attic bedroom watching the headlights of cars approaching the house, turning at the corner and disappearing, red taillights winking. Electronic tissue hum of the neural film projector.

Then I heard Pat moving, and her powerful image-energy machine flooded mine and I spun into her head. Gasping marshmallow flesh-fluff erotic jumping rapture.

Rumble seat sex. The dirty, skirty thirties. Who . . . means . . . your happiness . . . who . . . will you answer yes . . . who . . . well you ought to guess . . . who . . . no one but you . . . Pat's breath . . . whisky scented, fragile perfume of life . . . breath, air, sighing, air equals orgasm, air is life.

Sudden revelation into workings of oxygen monopoly. In the year 1888 British scientists, members of the Huxley family, discover that oxygen supply of earth is failing. Life, ecstasy, consciousness is oxygen. British aristocrats secretly bottle remaining vapours of air and hide it. Air is replaced by synthetic gas which possesses no life or consciousness, keeps people alive as plastic doll robots. Plump, mocking, effeminate, patronising Englishmen have control of precious oxygen elixir of life which they dole out in doses for their god-like amusement and pleasure. LSD is air.

The rest of the human race is doomed to three-D treadmill plastic repetition. Trapped. Oh, wise brown Ann who saw it all. I'd kill myself to end the meaningless rat race, but I'm afraid that wouldn't stop it. It would just spin out new and dead IBM sequences. My flesh, Pat and Parsons, the world was turning to dry brittle hardness.

Science-fiction horror. Hell! I wanted to shriek and run from the room for help. How to get back to life. Centre. Pray. Love. Touch. Contact. Human contact. Parsons, sloppy Jewish belly showing. Pat, swollen Jewish mother. I held on to her fat arm, burrowed into their body hive. We huddle in a heap on the floor in front of the fire, softly breathing together.

Spinning through sexual cellular scrapbooks. The eternal dance of male and female. The restless panting search. Sniffing search. Where is she? When will she come? The shock of contact. Soft flesh-furred, scaled, moist, merging. Ah there! Frantic, flailing, jumping, convulsive, moaning union. Breathless. Breathless. Chuckling she-wisdom. What else is important, you foolish desiccated creature, but this fire dance of life creation?

The murmuring giggling gooey: what else is immortal, oh dry brittle, save this moist buried flesh kiss?

For millennia I lay in geological trance. Forests grew on my flanks, rains came, continental ecstasies. Great slow heaving supporter of life. Vishnu sleeps and then from my bowel-centre-navel out grew the long slender green limb climbing up from the white-milk ocean of formlessness and completed the lotus blossom of awakedness.

I opened my eyes. I was in heaven. Illumination. Every object in the room was a radiant structure of atomic-god-like particles. Radiating. Matter did not exist. There was just this million-matrix lattice web of energies. Shimmering. Alive. Interconnected in space-time. Everything hooked up in a cosmic dance. Fragile. Indestructible.

And the incredible shattering discovery. Consciousness controlled it all. Or (to say it more accurately), all was consciousness.

I was staggered by the implication. All creation lay in front of me. I could live every life that had ever been lived, think every thought that had ever been thought. An endless variety of ecstatic experience spiralled out around me. I had taken the God-step.

I was dazed by the infinite permutations that offered themselves. Relive the life of Augustus Caesar. Relive the life of an illiterate untouchable in the squalor of an oriental city. Lives of history, lives of tedium.

A sudden thought. Now that this breakthrough of consciousness had occurred, a new level of harmony and love was available. I must bring my family, my friends to this new universe.

How simple and yet we almost missed it. Now that it's been done we can never lose it. How strange that I was the one to do it. And the endless possibilities. Each person had an endless supply of DNA memory file-cards collected during their tour down-there. The there world was a stage to create and collect fresh experience memory cards—now available for everyone up here in heaven.

THE JOYOUS COSMOLOGY

Alan Watts

Even before Leary began his work with psilocybin, Aldous Huxley had taken and written about mescaline and had gone on to explore the mysteries of LSD. Huxley was in touch with psychiatrists engaged in LSD research at the UCLA department of neuropsychology. It was to them that he sent his friend Alan Watts (1915–1973), who was interested in trying the drug. Watts's first trip was 'aesthetic rather than mystical', and he made a broadcast to this effect shortly afterwards. Watts had noticed a distinct change in Huxley's spiritual attitude after his drug experiences and had been hoping for a similar form of enlightenment. His broadcast was heard by two psychiatrists at the Langley-Porter Clinic in San Francisco, however, and they persuaded him to try again. The result was that Watts was 'reluctantly compelled to admit that—at least in my own case—LSD had brought me into an undeniably mystical state of consciousness'. It was these experiences that he recorded in The Joyous Cosmology *(1962), part of which is reprinted below.*

Alan Watts was born in England, at Chislehurst in Kent. He was educated at King's School, Canterbury, where he developed into something of a prodigy. At the age of fifteen he read Lafcadio Hearn's Glimpses of Unfamiliar Japan *and so began his life-long interest in Oriental religion and philosophy. While still at school he corresponded with leading Buddhists in England and published a booklet on Zen. After leaving school he became a committed Buddhist and studied under D. T. Suzuki and other leading teachers. In 1938 Watts married an American and, with war threatening Europe, they left to live in America. There he con-*

tinued to study and began to write the books which were to have such an immense influence on American youth. Strangely, Watts felt that he 'should find some way of fitting in with the traditions of Western culture', and in 1945 he was ordained as an Episcopalian priest. The move was a mistake and after five years he gave up the priesthood. He decided to 'live on his wits', making a living by writing and lecturing, because, as he said in his letter of resignation, 'I believe I have something to say that is worth saying.'

It is no coincidence that the subsequent popularity of Watts's books occurred simultaneously with the advent of LSD. His greatest gift was the ability to interpret Eastern religions for the Western layman, making a highly complex subject easily understandable. LSD promoted an enormous and extraordinary interest in these religions in America, a trend that had begun with Watts, and later with the writings of Gary Snyder, Jack Kerouac and Allen Ginsberg. Watts's books, among them The Way of Zen, Nature, Man and Woman, The Book on the Taboo Against Knowing Who You Are, Psychotherapy East and West *and, of course,* The Joyous Cosmology, *came to be found upon the bookshelves of every aspiring young American mystic. Watts himself attributed this explosion of interest in the mystical aspect of religion— triggered, as he says, by LSD—to 'increasing contact with Oriental cultures' and 'the arid theology and whipping-dead-horse preaching of standard-brand Judaism and Christianity'. He modestly failed to mention the fact that had there not been a brilliant, sympathetic and prolific teacher and explainer at hand—Watts himself—the explosion would have certainly been delayed and its impact probably halved. He continued his writing until the end of his life, publishing his autobiography* In My Own Way *in 1973, the year of his death.*

*   *   *

We each took one hundred micrograms of d-lysergic acid diethylamide-25, courtesy of the Sandoz company, and set out on an eight-hour exploration . . . Every detail of perception became vivid and

important, even ums and ers and throat-clearing when someone read
poetry, and time slowed down in such a way that people going about
their business seemed demented in failing to see that the destination of
life is this eternal moment ... At one time Edwin felt somewhat over-
whelmed and remarked, 'I just can't wait until I'm little old me again,
sitting in a bar.' In the meantime he was looking like an incarnation of
Apollo in a supernatural necktie, contemplatively holding an orange lily.

In My Own Way, 1973

I am listening to a priest chanting the Mass and a choir of nuns
responding. His mature, cultivated voice rings with the serene
authority of the One, Holy, Catholic and Apostolic Church, of
the Faith once and for all delivered to the saints, and the nuns
respond, naïvely it seems, with childlike, utterly innocent
devotion. But, listening again, I can hear the priest 'putting on'
his voice, hear the inflated, pompous balloon, the studiedly unctu-
ous tones of a master deceptionist who has the poor little nuns,
kneeling in their stalls, completely cowed. Listen deeper. The
nuns are not cowed at all. They are playing possum. With just a
little stiffening, the limp gesture of bowing turns into the gesture
of the closing claw. With too few men to go round, the nuns
know what is good for them: how to bend and survive.

But this profoundly cynical view of things is only an intermedi-
ate stage. I begin to congratulate the priest on his gamesmanship,
on the sheer courage of being able to put up such a performance
of authority when he knows precisely nothing. Perhaps there is
no other knowing than the mere competence of the act. If, at the
heart of one's being, there is no real self to which one ought to
be true, sincerity is simply nerve; it lies in the unabashed vigour
of the pretence.

But pretence is only pretence when it is assumed that the act
is not true to the agent. Find the agent. In the priest's voice I
hear down at the root the primordial howl of the beast in the
jungle, but it has been inflected, complicated, refined, and tex-
tured with centuries of culture. Every new twist, every additional
subtlety, was a fresh gambit in the game of making the original
howl more effective. At first, crude and unconcealed, the cry for
food or mate, or just noise for the fun of it, making the rocks
echo. Then rhythm to enchant, then changes of tone to plead or

threaten. Then words to specify the need, to promise and bargain. And then, much later, the gambits of indirection. The feminine stratagem of stooping to conquer, the claim to superior worth in renouncing the world for the spirit, the cunning of weakness proving stronger than the might of muscle—and the meek inheriting the earth.

As I listen, then, I can hear in that one voice the simultaneous presence of all the levels of man's history, as of all the stages of life before man. Every step in the game becomes as clear as the rings in a severed tree. But this is an ascending hierarchy of manoeuvres, of stratagems capping stratagems, all symbolised in the overlays of refinement beneath which the original howl is still sounding. Sometimes the howl shifts from the mating call of the adult animals to the helpless crying of the baby, and I feel all man's music—its pomp and circumstance, its gaiety, its awe, its confident solemnity—as just so much complication and concealment of baby wailing for mother. And as I want to cry with pity, I know I am sorry for myself. I, as an adult, am also back there alone in the dark, just as the primordial howl is still present beneath the sublime modulations of the chant.

You poor baby! And yet—you selfish little bastard! As I try to find the agent behind the act, the motivating force at the bottom of the whole thing, I seem to see only an endless ambivalence. Behind the mask of love I find my innate selfishness. What a predicament I am in if someone asks, 'Do you *really* love me?' I can't say yes without saying no, for the only answer that will really satisfy is, 'Yes I love you so much I could eat you! My love for you is identical with my love for myself. I love you with the purest selfishness.' No one wants to be loved out of a sense of duty.

So I will be very frank. 'Yes, I am pure, selfish desire and I love you because you make me feel wonderful—at any rate for the time being.' But then I begin to wonder whether there isn't something a bit cunning in this frankness. It is big of me to be so sincere, to make a play for her by not pretending to be more than I am—unlike the other guys who say they love her for herself. I see that there is always something insincere about trying to be sincere, as if I were to say openly, 'The statement that I am now making is a lie.' There seems to be something phoney about every attempt to define myself, to be totally honest. The trouble is that I can't see the back, much less the inside, of my head. I can't be honest because I don't fully know what I am. Consciousness peers out from a centre which it cannot see—and *that* is the root of the matter.

Life seems to resolve itself down to a tiny germ or nipple of sensitivity. I call it the Eenie-Weenie—a squiggling little nucleus that is trying to make love to itself and can never quite get there. The whole fabulous complexity of vegetable and animal life, as of human civilisation, is just a colossal elaboration of the Eenie-Weenie trying to make the Eenie-Weenie. I am in love with myself, but cannot seek myself without hiding myself. As I pursue my own tail, it runs away from me. Does the amoeba split itself in two in an attempt to solve this problem?

I try to go deeper, sinking thought and feeling down and down to their ultimate beginnings. What do I mean by loving *myself*? In what form do I know myself? Always, it seems, in the form of something other, something strange. The landscape I am watching is also a state of myself, of the neurons in my head. I feel the rock in my hand in terms of my own fingers. And nothing is stranger than my own body—the sensation of the pulse, the eye seen through a magnifying glass in the mirror, the shock of realising that oneself is something in the external world. At root, there is simply no way of separating self from other, self-love from other-love. All knowledge of self is knowledge of other, and all knowledge of other knowledge of self. I begin to see that self and other, the familiar and the strange, the internal and the external, the predictable and the unpredictable *imply* each other. One is seek and the other is hide, and the more I become aware of their implying each other, the more I feel them to be one with each other. I become curiously affectionate and intimate with all that seemed alien. In the features of everything foreign, threatening, terrifying, incomprehensible and remote I begin to recognise myself. Yet this is a 'myself' which I seem to be remembering from long, long ago—not at all my empirical ego of yesterday, not my specious personality.

The 'myself' which I am beginning to recognise, which I had forgotten but actually know better than anything else, goes far back beyond my childhood, beyond the time when adults confused me and tried to tell me that I was someone else; when, because they were bigger and stronger, they could terrify me with their imaginary fears and bewilder and outface me in the complicated game that I had not yet learned. (The sadism of the teacher explaining the game and yet having to prove his superiority in it.) Long before all that, long before I was an embryo in my mother's womb, there looms the ever-so-familiar stranger, the everything not me, which I recognise, with a joy immeasurably more intense than a meeting of lovers separated by centuries, to be my original self. The good old sonofabitch who got me involved in this whole game.

At the same time everyone and everything around me takes on the feeling of having been there always, and then forgotten, and then remembered again. We are sitting in a garden surrounded in every direction by uncultivated hills, a garden of fuchsias and hummingbirds in a valley that leads down to the westernmost ocean, and where the gulls take refuge in storms. At some time in the middle of the twentieth century, upon an afternoon in the summer, we are sitting round a table on the terrace, eating dark homemade bread and drinking white wine. And yet we seem to have been there forever, for the people with me are no longer the humdrum and harassed little personalities with names, addresses and social security numbers, the specifically dated mortals we are all pretending to be. They appear rather as immortal archetypes of themselves without, however, losing their humanity. It is just that their differing characters seem, like the priest's voice, to contain all history; they are at once unique and eternal, men and women but also gods and goddesses. For now that we have time to look at each other we become timeless. The human form becomes immeasurably precious and, as if to symbolise this, the eyes become intelligent jewels, the hair spun gold, and the flesh translucent ivory. Between those who enter

this world together there is also a love which is distinctly euchar-
istic, an acceptance of each other's natures from the heights to
the depths.

Ella, who planted the garden, is a beneficent Circe—sorceress,
daughter of the moon, familiar of cats and snakes, herbalist and
healer—with the youngest old face one has ever seen, exquisitely
wrinkled, silver-black hair rippled like flames. Robert is a manifestation of Pan, but a Pan of bulls instead of the Pan of goats,
with frizzled short hair tufted into blunt horns—a man all sweat-
ing muscle and body, incarnation of exuberant glee. Beryl, his
wife, is a nymph who has stepped out of the forest, a mermaid
of the land with swinging hair and a dancing body that seems to
be naked even when clothed. It is her bread that we are eating,
and it tastes like the Original Bread of which mother's own bread
was a bungled imitation. And then there is Mary, beloved in the
usual, dusty world, but in this world an embodiment of light and
gold, daughter of the sun, with eyes formed from the evening
sky—a creature of all ages, baby, moppet, maid, matron, crone
and corpse, evoking love of all ages.

I try to find words that will suggest the numinous, mythological
quality of these people. Yet at the same time they are as familiar
as if I had known them for centuries, or rather, as if I were
recognising them again as lost friends whom I knew at the beginning of time, from a country begotten before all worlds. This is
of course bound up with the recognition of my own most ancient
identity, older by far than the blind squiggling of the Eenie-
Weenie, as if the highest form that consciousness could take had
somehow been present at the very beginning of things. All of us
look at each other knowingly, for the feeling that we knew each
other in that most distant past conceals something else—tacit,
awesome, almost unmentionable—the realisation that at the deep
centre of a time perpendicular to ordinary time we are, and always
have been, one. We acknowledge the marvellously hidden plot,
the master illusion, whereby we appear to be different.

The shock of recognition. In the form of everything most other,
alien, and remote—the ever-receding galaxies, the mystery of
death, the terrors of disease and madness, the foreign-feeling,

gooseflesh world of sea-monsters and spiders, the queasy laby-
rinth of my own insides—in all these forms I have crept up on
myself and yelled 'Boo!' I scare myself out of my wits, and,
while out of my wits, cannot remember just how it happened.
Ordinarily I am lost in a maze. I don't know how I got here, for
I have lost the thread and forgotten the intricately convoluted
system of passages through which the game of hide-and-seek
was pursued. (Was it the path I followed in growing the circuits
of my brain?) But now the principle of the maze is clear. It is
the device of something turning back upon itself so as to seem
to be other, and the turns have been so many and so dizzyingly
complex that I am quite bewildered. The principle is that all
dualities and opposites are not disjoined but polar; they do not
encounter and confront one another from afar; they exfoliate
from a common centre. Ordinary thinking conceals polarity and
relativity because it employs *terms*, the terminals or ends, the
poles, neglecting what lies between them. The difference of front
and back, to be and not to be, hides their unity and mutuality.

Now consciousness, sense perception, is always a sensation of
contrasts. It is a specialisation in differences, in noticing, and
nothing is definable, classifiable or noticeable except by contrast
with something else. But man does not live by consciousness
alone, for the linear, step-by-step, contrast-by-contrast procedure
of attention is quite inadequate for organising anything so complex as a living body. The body itself has an 'omniscience' which
is unconscious, or superconscious, just because it deals with
relation instead of contrast, with harmonies rather than discords.
It 'thinks' or organises as a plant grows, not as a botanist describes
its growth. This is why Shiva has ten arms, for he represents the
dance of life, the omnipotence of being able to do innumerably
many things at once.

In the type of experience I am describing, it seems that the
superconscious method of thinking becomes conscious. We see
the world as the whole body sees it, and for this very reason
there is the greatest difficulty in attempting to translate this mode
of vision into a form of language that is based on contrast and
classification. To the extent, then, that man has become a being

centred in consciousness, he has become centred in clash, conflict and discord. He ignores, as beneath notice, the astounding perfection of his organism as a whole, and this is why, in most people, there is such a deplorable disparity between the intelligent and marvellous order of their bodies and the trivial preoccupations of their consciousness. But in this other world the situation is reversed. Ordinary people look like gods because the values of the organism are uppermost, and the concerns of consciousness fall back into the subordinate position which they should properly hold. Love, unity, harmony and relationship therefore take precedence over war and division.

For what consciousness overlooks is the fact that all boundaries and divisions are held in common by their opposite sides and areas, so that when a boundary changes its shape both sides move together. It is like the *yang-yin* symbol of the Chinese—the black and white fishes divided by an S-curve inscribed within a circle. The bulging head of one is the narrowing tail of the other. But how much more difficult it is to see that my skin and its movements belong both to me and to the external world, or that the spheres of influence of different human beings have common walls like so many rooms in a house, so that the movement of my wall is also the movement of yours. You can do what you like in your room just so long as I can do what I like in mine. But each man's room is himself in his fullest extension, so that my expansion is your contraction and vice versa.

GOOD OLE CAGEY CAGE

William J. Craddock

'Does it ever wear off, man?'

'Not completely, but it fades. How'd you like it?'

Nothing to say but, 'Wow.'

'Yup, that's what everybody says.'

It imploded in my stomach, bowels and head at the same time. I could talk to this person. He understood. It was real! The experience was as big as I thought it was. Others had seen it. The shared wow—the sacred wow.

The passage above is from Be Not Content *by William J. Craddock (1940–   ). The protagonist, Abel Egregore, having taken LSD for the first time, has just met someone else who has undergone the same experience, the same feeling of 'wow'.* Be Not Content, *to quote the book's one-sentence blurb, is a 'skeletal history and chronicle of the experiences of a single, minor freak connected to a single, minor tribe of acid freaks in California, beginning in the early days of the Psychedelic Revolution, including a brief sampling of the insignificant individuals involved, their ideas and ideals, and a flickering glimpse of but a scant few of the problems, obstacles, superstitions, fears, misunderstandings, joys, insights, loves and frustrations that they faced, manufactured and struggled with in their once pure quest for the elusive path to even more enlightenment in a set constructed exclusively of intricate but obvious illusions of which they occasionally (with infinite sadness, regretting the revelation) realised that they were undeniably a micro-part.' The sweet sadness of this description is shared by the book itself; it chronicles*

Abel's passage from the early, euphoric days when LSD arrived, a miracle substance to cleanse and awaken its users, to the disillusionment and disgust of 1967 when LSD was discovered by the eager media, the 'Summer of Love' was manufactured, packaged and sold, and Haight-Ashbury became a living hell. Be Not Content *is a depressing but strangely neglected and important book.*

Its importance lies in its description of the early days of the 'psychedelic revolution' as seen by an ordinary young Californian. Abel is not an Alan Watts or a Timothy Leary. He is a young man with no interest in mysticism, with no intellectual pretensions, who first takes LSD for 'kicks'. Once he has taken the drug, however, he is forced to reconstruct his life and embarks on a quest for 'elusive enlightenment'. In the course of the book he travels through all the pains and pleasures of LSD, sensations now familiar to millions; but Abel is a pioneer in uncharted territory, with only his friends, equally inexperienced, as companions.

William J. Craddock was born and educated in California, and for a time rode with Hell's Angels. Be Not Content *was his first book and there is an obvious affinity between it and Kerouac's work. Although it is classed as non-fiction,* Be Not Content *reads as a novel and, like Kerouac's* On the Road *or* The Dharma Bums, *transforms autobiographical material with 'real' people into a fictional form. Also, like Kerouac, his drug experience affects the structure and style of his writing. As Kerouac used the long, rambling, stream-of-consciousness form to capture Neal Cassady's amphetamine monologues, so Craddock manipulates the traditional form of the book in order to convey something of the change in one's view of time and space that occurs after LSD.*

The chapter I have reprinted here is only partially representative of the book as a whole. I have chosen it, however, because it conveys brilliantly the atmosphere of euphoria that existed in California before LSD was declared illegal in October 1966, and the resultant climate of paranoia and police harassment.

*   *   *

These are words about the early morning witnessed by some people who
came to be known as 'hippies'. It's a collection of words written in acid.
It isn't a 'hip' collection of words. There are no 'hip' collections of words.
All word-collections are only words. The wisest collections (among them
the Christian Bible, beyond all its padding and bullshit) tell us that once
there *were* no words, the time will come when there *will* be no words,
and in actuality, there *are* no words.

Be Not Content, 1970

I slid the door open and Preston grinned at me, match already
to joint, thrusting a newspaper at my face with his free hand.
On the front page the headlines announced, MOTORCYCLE
DOPE-RING LEADER ARRESTED, and below and to the right
of the heavy black words was a fine photograph of our old buddy,
Roy Cage. 'They got ole Cagey,' said Preston. 'Motorcycle dope-
ring leader that he is.'

I read the article while Preston made himself a cup of instant
coffee. Cage had been arrested after he'd foolishly befriended a
teenage, flower-child chick who was later picked up for 'being
in danger of leading a loose and immoral life', freaked out and
pointed the finger at Cage as the source of her corruption and a
big-time dope-dealer. 'They got good ole Cagey Cage.'

I finished the newspaper story, which stated that Leroy David
Cage was a member of the *Hell's Angels* (untrue) and the leader
of a statewide dope-ring (also untrue), turned back to page one
and studied Cage's picture. Cage with his hair and beard all
snarled and wild (they broke into his cabin while he was asleep),
looking like a wise-guy Christ on the cross, his shoulders bare,
mouth a tight line but his eyes prankster-smiling the way they
always did, gold chain around his neck with just the top of its
crucifix visible in the photo. It's Cage all right.

'You realise, of course, Preston, that Cage isn't going to stand
for this. He's undoubtedly let it go this far only because "They
know not what they do." '

'Right,' said Preston, gulping down his coffee and passing the
joint, 'I just hope he doesn't go too easy on the fuckers.'

The rest of the day was set aside for heavy sacrament smoking
and reminiscing in honour of captured Roy Cage.

Cage was a mountain-boy who ran full tilt, head up and grinning, through a fast early teens of stealing cars and smashing them into trees with the law in hot pursuit over winding mountain roads that Roy knew far better than any sheriff. He bought an old '39 Indian motor-cycle when he was about fifteen, and rattled over hills and highways at unbelievable speeds, flying off embankments and into fences regularly, having a good mountain-boy time in general.

He turned on to weed before long, and then turned all of his Okie and hill-folk pals on to it. For an impossible couple of years, he and his wild followers did things like getting drunk on wine, then high on weed to drive their lumbering old Cadillacs, Buicks, Chevies and worn-out Studebakers into a parking-lot where they'd hold destruction derbys, driving foot-to-the-floor-flat-out and howling with mad laughter into one another until all the cars were dead, then they'd hitchhike home.

Cage gave up stealing cars, wrecking cars, and berserk activities when he became fantastically devoted to marijuana. He once had a photograph taken of his '52 Chevie covered with all the weed he and his friends could get their hands on (nearly a hundred keys), while he stood on the top with a pitchfork in one hand. He wanted to have post-cards made from the picture to send to friends, but then decided that they might fall into the wrong hands and 'tend to criminate' him.

When acid became available, he took it and arrived at the conclusion that he was God. His mountain-boy followers (as well as a few hip city people who took acid with him for a laugh and got more than they bargained for) became his disciples and actually sat at his feet while he told them how nice it was going to be when they finally all got together and broke on through to The Kingdom.

'Can I have me a '63 Cor-vette, Cage?'

'Anything you want, Russ. You jus want it an it's right there.'

Once, he just dug in with a tablespoon and ate some unknown and unbelievable quantity of acid that was sitting in a bowl waiting to be capped. When it came on, he started controlling the universe. Days passed with Cage bringing the sun up on time, making it go across the sky, pushing it down behind the hills and calling for night, lighting all the stars, seeing that people and animals went to sleep and continued to breathe while they were unconscious, tending to the wind, making trees and flowers grow, causing the world to turn at just the right speed.

On the fourth day, Cage got tired and wanted to sleep himself, but by now he had too many obligations.

'There wasn't hardly no moon las'night, Cage.'

'I know, but I got a lot on muh mind. You're lucky there was a moon atal.'

On the sixth day, Cage was so tired that he decided to let the universe take its chances for a few hours while he rested. He closed his eyes, started to drop off . . . and his heart stopped. When his heart stopped, so did the universe. To start his heart— and thereby keep the universe in order—he had to walk. One step—one heart-beat—one breath—one click of the universe-cog. Another step—another heart-beat—exhale—one more click of the big cog . . . for five hours, and then he got panicky.

'Well . . . I wasn't really *panicked* like. I wuz just kinda concerned.'

Racking his very busy brain for a way out, he hit upon the idea of calling the Stanford Research Center on the phone.

'I knew there wuz alota smart people up there cuz I read about it once.'

He had to march in place while he was on the phone.

'I tole em what ma problem wuz an said they'd better help me out if they wanted to keep on wakin up in the mornins, but they jus tole me I'd been messin where I shouldna been an to go to sleep. They wuzn't so smart as I read they wuz. They almos ended the whole world right there.'

Luckily, Cage discovered by himself how to put 'the whole works on remote-automatic-control', and he finally went to bed. Unfortunately, 'remote-automatic-control' was 'only good for maybe eight hours. Then she heats up.' The universe was still in his hands.

Cage got all his pals high on acid and then delegated responsibilities by granting them special powers for a limited amount of time.

'I knew I could do it, cuz one time I said ''Norm, you got the power to go get me a drinka water'' . . . and he done it right off.'

'Fred,' he'd say, 'I'm gonna let you work the sun for awhile. Now don't you go screwin it up.' Fred would sit down immediately and carefully concentrate on running the sun, honoured by Cage's trust in him and well aware of the importance of this cosmic task. Then Cage would give other jobs like wind, earth-turning, clouds, etc. to other responsible disciples, watch them for a while to make sure they had the hang of it, then slip away for a quick, much deserved nap.

Even those of us who didn't necessarily believe that Cage was God and in control of the cosmos (although he might well have been) liked to go up and visit him. His exploits had, by this time, made him almost a legendary figure among local psychedelic pioneers.

'I read where you can buy this pickled head,' he told Baxtor and I. 'I'm gonna get me that head,' he said slowly, rubbing his bearded chin and working out the details as he spoke, 'I'm gonna put it behind these . . . like curtains, see? an then maybe put all kindsa screams and moans on this tape recorder. Then I'm gonna get a buncha mah partners together an give em all a big dose a acid an sit em down in fronta these curtains an tell em this story 'bout the head and how there's this curse on it an anybody who looks at this head goes nuts right off. Then I say that *I* got the head an here it is right here, and then I pull back the curtains an play the screams an stuff.' He chuckled his deep, Cage chuckle, visualising the scene. 'That'd sure put a few of em in the hospital. Yessir, there'd sure be alota blowed-out minds aroun here if I done that.'

Cage began reading for the first time in his life after he took acid. He read whatever was lying around—comic books, novels, magazines, old textbooks, anything, because it was all new to him. Somebody left him some books on Tibet and he devoured them in one sitting, shooting crink to keep his eyes open.

'I think I oughta go to Tibet,' he said a week or so later. 'I wanna meet up with one a them hermit monks I read about. Ya know, they can jus make anythin they want outta thin air. Jus

... zap ... an it's right there. They wear these robes an that's
how they get em. Right outta thin air. I'm gonna go to Tibet an
look one a these cats up an have im take me to their hang-out
and get em all t'gether—maybe lay a couple of caps a acid on
em—an tell em I got alota power an wanna join up with them.
Then I'll say, "Let's see what you can do" an ask em to make
me up a robe outta thin air. Not jus *any* robe. I'll tell em to get
me Christ's robe. I'd sure like to come on back from Tibet wearin
Christ's robe.'

Baxtor pursed his lips and said, 'I don't know, Cage. Those
monks are pretty clannish. They might not accept a Western
sage.'

Cage considered this unforeseen hangup, squinting his eyes
and scratching his beard. 'Well,' he said, 'then I'll haveta start
up mah own buncha hermit monks an wipe them other ones out.'

Cage grew quieter and deeper as time went by and he digested
more and more acid. Too old and wise at twenty-three to steal
and punch cops and raise hell or even get drunk with his partners,
he settled down to selling weed and acid, reading books he found
and developing 'The Power'. He quit worrying about making a
profit on the dope he sold and gave it away or passed it on for
pretty much what it cost him. 'I'm jus spreadin the word,' he'd
smile. 'I ain't no dope dealer. I'm a missionary ... workin on
bein a Messiah.'

'I always knew they'd eventually get ole Cagey Cage,' said
Preston when we'd gone over Cage's countless adventures for
the third time, 'Remember when he had this plan to get the
smallest man in the world—some little dwarf he'd read about in
one of those magazines of his—and put him in a glass case so
he could watch him and smoke weed with him? And then he was
going to invite the tallest man in the world over for dinner and
introduce the two freaks to one another to see "how they hit it
off".'

I remember. I also remember, 'That time we all went to the
beach with him to dig that eclipse of the moon, and the whole
thing really got to ole Cage an he wrote that message in the
sand—huge letters, saying, "GOD ... IMPORTANT. GET IN

TOUCH WITH ME . . .'' with his phone-number under it.'

Preston picked up the newspaper and looked at the headlines and Cage's picture again. '*Motorcycle dope-ring leader*. It *is* rewarding. Local boy makes good.'

Roy Cage, missionary working on being a Messiah, went to prison and wasn't to come out for two years.

So many friends sent to prisons and work-farms and jails as felons for owning ounces of dried-up weed. People walking around free on the outside, plotting ways to cheat their neighbours, planning wars, making money on alcohol-drug and diet-drug and nicotine-drug, polluting the oceans and rivers and the air, lie-makers and hate-makers and walking-death-merchants all free to come and go, seeing nothing but one side of their green-paper-money blindfold, while inside prisons gentle friends are made to stare at steel bars and grey stone walls because they took it all seriously and wanted to talk to God.

A TRIP TO STONESVILLE

Andrew Weil

While Timothy Leary was doing his pioneer research at Harvard in the early Sixties, Andrew Weil (1942–   ) was a student at the university. Already fascinated by Huxley's remarks on the mescaline experience, Weil, who was studying biology, asked Leary if he could be a subject in the psychologist's psilocybin experiments. Leary refused, as he was not allowed to use students in drug experiments. In 1961 Weil managed to get some mescaline, but he was disappointed with the experience at first. However, he remained fascinated by the whole field of consciousness change and continued to study it while at Harvard's medical school. In 1967, at the end of his course, he decided to conduct a double-blind human study of marijuana. (It is, of course, astounding that one had not been conducted before and that it should take a young, enthusiastic medical student to instigate such a study.) After meeting great hostility from the authorities, Weil finally conducted his study, with the help of Norman Zinberg and Judith Nelsen. The resultant article, 'Clinical and Psychological Effects of Marijuana in Man', published in 1968, remains one of the crucial studies of the drug. 'In retrospect,' Weil has written, 'I think the most important result of our work was simply the demonstration that it was possible to administer marijuana to human volunteers in a laboratory, obtain usable results, and get away with it.'

The study established Weil as one of the foremost medical authorities on marijuana in the world. He continued to study consciousness-changing drugs, working for a time at the Haight-Ashbury Medical Clinic, and as he studied drugs and drug users one of his early beliefs was confirmed: that man has an innate need to change his own consciousness periodically. This is first manifested by such childhood pursuits as spinning round and round until giddy, and such 'adult' pursuits as drinking oneself into a stupor. The confirmation of this belief was to form the foundation of his book The Natural Mind *(1972).*

It is a remarkable book, not easy to summarise in a few sentences; I hope that the excerpt reprinted below will convey something of its flavour and argument. In The Natural Mind *Weil compares 'straight thinking'—that engaged in by everybody sometimes, and by those in power in Western society most of the time—which sees* either/or, *to 'stoned thinking' which sees* both/ and. *Straight thinking is straight 'in the way an interstate highway is straight; unlike a winding country road it does not follow the natural contours of reality. And in its ever-widening divergence from reality it leads straight to impotence, despair and death . . .' Stoned thinking entails an extension of consciousness and an openness to non-ordinary reality. It is adaptable, non-linear and intuitive. Drugs are an aid to achieving stoned thinking. Weil sees drugs as 'active placebos' and believes that theyhelp the user to break through to 'spontaneous highs'. Once he can become high spontaneously and reach a state approximate to that which was once the exclusive property of the mystics, then he can discard drugs. Unfortunately, most people* will *need drugs to reach such a state. It is therefore wrong—and even suicidal— to try to stamp out 'the drug problem'. If we continue to fight drugs then 'they will grow ever more destructive. Accept them and they can be turned into nonharmful, even beneficial forces.'*

In recent years Weil has come to be regarded as a guru on alternative lifestyles and is frequently referred to in the press as a 'pioneer of Medicine of the Future'. He now lives in Arizona, where he founded the Centre for Integrative Medicine at Tucson, and writes best-selling books on health such as Eight Weeks to Optimum Health *(1997).*

*   *   *

It is my belief that the desire to alter consciousness periodically is an innate, normal drive analogous to hunger or the sexual drive. Note that I do not say 'desire to alter consciousness by means of chemical agents.' Drugs are merely one way of satisfying this drive; there are many others . . .

The Natural Mind, 1972

Stoned thinking is the mirror image of straight thinking. When we step into nonordinary reality even for a moment, we experience things directly, see inner contents rather than external forms, and suddenly find ourselves able to participate in changing things for the better. This other way of interpreting perceptions comes first as episodic flashes, unpredictable, discontinuous. But the more flashes of it one has, the easier it becomes to maintain. And stoned thinking is not something foreign to be learned; it develops spontaneously as we unlearn habitual ways of using the mind.

It would be absurd to attempt to describe a way of thinking based in experience rather than description. Therefore, I will keep my comments about stoned thinking to a minimum and instead will give a number of examples of conceptions it has led me to over the past few years. As briefly as possible, here are the essential components of the process:

1   *Reliance on intuition as well as intellection*
Intuition is something known to all of us by experience; to the intellect it is a mystery. In fact, intellectual speculation about the nature of intuition is in the same muddle it was when it started, many years ago. Contemporary educational theorists recognise that intuition is the most important intrinsic factor governing acquisition of information in the growing child, but I am not impressed that they have developed effective methods of fostering this capacity in the process of education.

Intuitive flashes are transient, spontaneous altered states of consciousness consisting of particular sensory experiences or thoughts coupled with strong emotional reactions. But—and this is the distinguishing feature—the intellect cannot explain the association; there is no logical reason for the feelings we get on meeting certain persons, places, things, or ideas. Such real experiences, being nonordinary, challenge the logic of ordinary consciousness. So, in our ordinary waking state, we are uneasy about intuitive knowledge and, consequently, unable to describe it well, predict it well, or control it well.

If our ordinary conscious minds have no record of associations between certain experiences and certain feelings, where do these associations originate? They originate in the unconscious mind, and the strangeness of intuitions is the same strange feeling we experience whenever a portion of our unconscious life breaks through to our waking awareness. This sense of the nonordinary is strongest when it accompanies the purest forms of intuitions: unaccountable yet powerful convictions of knowing how things really are—of sensing directly that something is true. Probably, all people have such intuitions from time to time, but only some people act on them or bother to check on their usefulness. That is to say, only some of us trust our intuitions.

Now, the history of science makes clear that the greatest advancements in man's understanding of the universe are made by intuitive leaps at the frontiers of knowledge, not by intellectual walks along well-travelled paths. Similarly, the greatest scientific thinkers are those who rely on sudden intuitive flashes to solve problems. Nevertheless, all of our universities attempt to train scientists by methods appropriate to the development of the intellect rather than the intuitive faculty.

In considering straight thinking, we noted that the essence of intellection is inductive reasoning: that is, the elaboration of general hypotheses from specific data provided by the senses. We saw also that the problem with total reliance on this process is the danger of formulating hypotheses divergent from reality, failing to prove them by actual experiment, and using them as premises for subsequent reasoning and action. Teaching in science today relies exclusively on inductive procedures. For example, the entire preclinical curriculum of medical school is a mass of specific facts, observations and experimental data, from which students of allopathy are expected to draw general conclusions regarding health and illness.

The looking-glass version of this process is deduction—that

is, reasoning away from general premises to the specific case at hand. If the premises are known to be sound, the conclusions will be sound, too. And our intuitive faculty is nothing other than a source of sound premises about the nature of reality.

Learning to be stoned (or unlearning to be straight) does not mean rejecting the intellect (a mistake made by some persons who wake up to the nature of straight thinking, then devote all of their energies to fighting it rather than developing a positive alternative). As a machine for producing thoughts, the intellect has a useful function if it is put in its proper place. And that place is coordinate with the intuitive faculty. As we become aware of our intuitions, learn to trust them, and then feed them into our intellects as premises, we begin to come up with very interesting and very useful ideas to guide us—useful because they lead us towards reality rather than away from it.

This guiding function of intuition has been venerated by wise men throughout history. They have told us again and again, in legends and myths, aphorisms, poems and allegories that there exists within us a source of direct information about reality that can teach us all we need to know. (Which is, after all, the literal meaning of the word *intuition*.) Maimonides called this source 'the still, small voice'. A Chinese sage, Hsuan-chiao, said of it: 'You remain silent and it speaks,/You speak and it is silent.' many commentators call it superconsciousness to distinguish it from the 'lower' (or subconscious) functions of the unconscious mind, such as the operation of the autonomic nervous system. And all of them stress that the only requirement for getting in touch with this source is the suspension of ordinary mental activity. We cannot make intuitions happen; we can only let them enter our awareness. In fact, if we disengage our awareness from ego consciousness and intellect, we cannot stop intuitive knowledge from bubbling up out of the unconscious depths. In daydreams, trances, reveries, meditations, we are much more open to our unconscious mind and to the inner teachings that come through it. And this openness obtains regardless of the means used to enter the altered states of consciousness. It is important to understand that the drug subculture in America, despite much superficial antiintellectualism, is providing many young people with social support for becoming aware of and trusting their own intuitions—something the dominant culture has failed to do.

Coordination of intellection with intuition with increased reliance on deductive reasoning is the outstanding characteristic of stoned thinking. The other characteristics I will now mention follow from this first because they are really based on specific intuitions that come to us when we leave ordinary consciousness behind.

2   Acceptance of the ambivalent nature of things

Ambivalence is the coexistence of opposites that appear to be mutually antagonistic. Straight thinking with its either/or logic cannot understand this phenomenon, much less accept it and derive benefit from it. But as soon as we tune out of our intellects and into our intuitive sources of knowledge, we discover that ambivalence is part of the way things are. In commenting on the 'universal law of coexisting opposites,' Heinrich Zimmer, an Oriental scholar, has written: '. . . completeness consists in opposites cooperating through conflict . . . the pattern of existence is woven of antagonistic cooperation, alternations of ascendancy and decline . . . it is built of bright *and* dark, day *and* night— *Yang* and *Yin*, in the Chinese formulation.'

The idea that reality manifests itself to us in the guise of pairs of opposites is a very old one. It appears frequently in Oriental philosophies and religions, and in the Western tradition is traceable back to the Garden of Eden, where it takes the form of the Tree of Knowledge of Good and Evil. Modern physicists have pursued this paradoxical dualism into the subatomic world, where they find that entities like electrons and photons can exist either as waves or particles, energy or matter.

The problem is not that things have this ambivalent nature, but that our ordinary consciousness cannot accept it. Stoned consciousness, however, is perfectly capable of substituting a both/ and formation for the either/or of the ego. In fact, in altered states of consciousness people often experience pairs of opposites simultaneously and find the experience very worthwhile.

Here is a mundane example: some years ago I took a dose of LSD in Death Valley on a night of the full moon in July. One of my most vivid recollections of the night is that I could not tell whether I was warm or cold because I had both sensations simultaneously and powerfully. Furthermore, this simultaneous experience of opposite sensations was intimately bound up with a state of egolessness, timelessness, and tremendously increased ability to concentrate. I do not believe these effects were pharmacological; I have experienced them since that time without having taken any drug.

The point is that when we enter nonordinary reality, our relationship to the pairs of opposites changes. Instead of trying to hold one and shun the other, we are able to transcend both, to experience them as two phases of manifestation of a single reality. This experience wipes out many straight notions and thereby solves many problems, because many problems are rooted in the ego's conception of reality rather than in reality itself. For example, the whole mind-body problem that has stimulated such an outflow of straight prose becomes a problem only by thinking of it as such. The statement of the question limits the possible information one can get in an answer because it presupposes a meaningful distinction between the two phases of perceiving a single reality. Mind and body are really the two expressions of the same phenomenon—just as waves and particles are two phases of expression of the entity called an electron.

Niels Bohr named the relationship between these two phases. He called it 'complementarity.' Bohr did not extend his understanding of an aspect of the nature of physical reality to all of human experience. But a contemporary chemist wrote in *Science* in 1971: 'It is conceivable . . . that the notion of complementarity offers a method of including both sensuous [i.e., experiential] and intellectual knowledge in a common frame of reference.' Being stoned is simply experiencing directly this single frame of reference—this one reality with its endlessly oscillating phases of wave/particle, light/dark, mind/body.

Unitive consciousness is the precise goal of all religions and philosophies of mind development. It is also the philosophers' stone of alchemists, at least of the less materialistic ones, which makes the term *stoned consciousness* perfectly appropriate. And one method of approaching the goal, all of these systems tell us, is by not trying to cling to one phase and avoid the other. Thus, Lao Tzu writes of the *Way of Life*:

> One who, preferring light,
> Prefers darkness also
> Is in himself an image of the world
> And, being an image of the world,
> Is continuously, endlessly
> The dwelling of creation.

And in the *Bhagavad-Gita*, Krishna says:

> Feelings of heat and cold, pleasure and pain are caused by the contact of the senses with their objects. They come and they go, never lasting long. You must accept them.
>   A serene spirit accepts pleasure and pain with an even mind and is unmoved by either. He alone is worthy of immortality.

Probably, there are many valid techniques for achieving this kind of detachment. One method, a classical one, is to reach equilibrium by experiencing opposites simultaneously. Any quality can be neutralised by combining it with its opposite in equal strength; the principle applies to love and hate as well as to positron and electron. And, although the cancellation of opposites leads to the state designated mathematically by the zero sign, the actual experience of this state is not of nothingness but of everythingness. For this reason, stoned thinking leads also to:

3   *Experience of infinity in its positive aspect*
Whether we realise it or not, many of us have experienced infinity, but to ordinary consciousness the experience is intensely negative. I will give a personal example.

In 1964, when I was a senior in college, I took a large dose (40 milligrams) of psilocybin. At that time I did not understand hallucinogens well enough to control them; nor did I know enough about set and setting to be able to shape the experience to the form I wanted it to take. I took the drug in a college dormitory room. Twenty minutes later, I suddenly began to experience striking visual illusions that became more and more kaleidoscopic. In one hour, my experience of reality had become completely fragmented, especially my intellectual experience, and since, as a good Harvard man, I was unable to detach myself from my intellect, the day became more and more unpleasant. The essence of this unpleasantness was symbolised by a recurring visual illusion and memory—the memory of sitting in barbers' chairs as a child, transfixed with the infinite regressions of mirrors facing each other. With a too large dose of psilocybin, this same infinite regression burst in on every sense channel, and I had no way of orientating (or anchoring) myself in the ordinary reality in which I could communicate to others. My intellect was so affected that every time it produced a thought, it would automatically think about the thought, think about thinking about the thought, and so on down the tunnel of mirrors. The more I tried to use my intellect to get me out of the expanding confusion, the more dimensions the confusion assumed.

I survived the storm, coming out of it after several hours with only a bad headache. I have not made the same mistakes again, and I think I have profited greatly from the experience. For one thing, it enabled me to see that all panic reactions to drugs (and, I suspect, to psychosis) in which patients think they are losing their minds have at their heart this negative experience of infinity; having had the experience myself, I am now able to help others out of it. Also, it unstraightened my thinking by showing me starkly the inability of my intellect to deal with infinity, which, intuition tells me, is surely an aspect of reality.

Just as we live in a universe where single realities express themselves in two opposite polarities or valences, so also we live in an infinite universe where everything is relative. At every step in the development of human consciousness, men have described limits to things only to have those limits exploded by subsequent experience of things beyond. Indeed, the history of astronomy from ancient Greece to the present is a continuing saga of an expanding universe—expanding in the conceptions of men. And try as we will with straight thinking to banish the notion of infinity, it keeps breaking in—in the heavens, in the subatomic world, and, of course, in the barber's shop. I think there is no need to add that every religion uses the term *infinite* to describe its highest conception, or that all mystics have seen infinity wherever they looked. (Aldous Huxley took the title for his essay on mescaline from the following line of William Blake: 'If the doors of perception were cleansed, every thing would appear to man as it is—infinite.')

The ego can see infinity only in its threatening aspect (that is, threatening to the ego's limited world). Consequently, the ordinary experience of infinity, if intense enough, is always accompanied by negative emotions and often by physical symptoms such as nausea (a very particular unpleasant sensation distinguished by its wavelike quality). To defend itself from these assaults, the intellect often tells us that the concept of infinity is meaningless or incomprehensible. And so it is, like every other mystery that can only be experienced directly. Only in nonordinary consciousness can we experience the looking-glass version of infinity—in which the same perceptions evoke strongly positive reactions. The more we strive to extend and maintain awareness of our flashes of stoned thinking, the more we can experience infinity positively, accept it, derive strength from it, and incorporate it consciously into our lives, thus decreasing the divergence between reality and our conceptions of it.

In this way, stoned thinking leads us out of the predicament of straight thinking. As our conceptions come to fit reality better, action taken from those conceptions produces the effects we want instead of the reverse. Rather than fighting negative manifestations of nature (and thereby making them assume worse forms), we are suddenly able to transform negative things into positive things. Just as negative thinking is self-confirming, so is positive thinking; in sustained periods of stoned consciousness the sense that things are getting better and better is overwhelming—at least as powerful as the ego's conviction of imminent disaster. And a great deal of this optimism arises directly from one of the clearest messages coming across the intuitive channel: that there are no limits. The only limits we encounter in the world around us are those we first create in our imagination.

3

Maybe if you were not so afraid of becoming mad, or of losing your body, you would understand this marvellous secret. But perhaps you must wait until you lose your fear to understand what I mean.

The Teachings of Don Juan: A Yaqui Way of Knowledge,
CARLOS CASTANEDA, 1968

All the writers so far represented have been American by birth or by adoption. It would be foolish to pretend that the greatest post-World War II developments in the field of drug-inspired literature have not taken place in the United States; it would be equally foolish to deny that work of the highest standard has been done outside America.

During the 1950s and '60s the energy centre was undoubtedly California. In this third part, however, I wish to represent five writers working outside California. Three are Americans, one is Belgian and the other is British. The first American, Paul Bowles, can be considered an honorary Moroccan for he has lived in that country since the war and his work is steeped in the life and culture of North Africa. Terry Southern cannot be classified in geographical terms, but the story here represents a drug vision that is firmly based in the milieu of New York. Michaux, a Belgian, was a compulsive traveller—particularly in the remote parts of South America—and a lifelong student of consciousness change. Alexander Trocchi, a Scotsman, also travelled very widely and wrote from an almost global viewpoint, as does another expatriate American, Brion Gysin.

The United States is the world's prime example of a drug culture. Drugs pervade every level of the country's life. For this reason alone it will no doubt remain the focal point of the tradition for many years to come. Past experience, however, indicates that sooner or later a group of writers will emerge in another place to push the boundaries outward yet again. Changing one's consciousness by chemical means is a practice as old as man himself;

but every day new information is being discovered, new drugs are being used. Many questions persist and doubtless much experimentation is still required to find the answers. It remains uncertain whether society will decree that they must continue to be found in secrecy or in the light of public acceptance.

THE WIND AT BENI MIDAR

Paul Bowles

*It is perhaps most appropriate to begin this section with a story
from one of the 'cradles' of drug usage, Morocco in North Africa,
as this serves to underline the continuing tradition which we have
examined in this anthology. The use of cannabis is deeply ingrained
in the fabric of the country, yet it still holds many secrets for all its
users. One writer who has lived and worked in Morocco for many
years and has seen and absorbed much of this atmosphere is the
American novelist,* Paul Bowles *(1910–   ). The people and the
customs of the country permeate most of his work, and his deep
knowledge of, and insight into, drug experience are to be found in
several memorable stories such as 'The Story of Lahcen and Idir'
and 'The Wind at Beni Midar', which is included here.*

*Paul Bowles was born in New York, but spent much of his early
life either studying literature and music in Europe or wandering
across four continents. He won early acclaim for his compositions
and has scored operas, ballets and many films, including such
diverse productions as Shakespeare's* Twelfth Night *and* The Glass
Menagerie *by Tennessee Williams. His first novel,* The Sheltering
Sky, *was published in 1949; it immediately established him as a
major writer, and subsequent volumes such as* Let It Come Down,
Up Above the World *and the collection of short stories,* Pages from
Cold Point, *have served to underline this position. In the story
reprinted here he draws upon a wealth of personal memories to
paint a bizarre fantasy complete with* kif *visions and mystic figures.*

*   *   *

His custom was not to smoke kif before the sun went down. He did not like it in the daytime, above all in the summer when the air is hot and the light is powerful. When each day came up hotter than the one before it, he decided to buy enough food and kif to last several days, and to shut himself into his room until it got cooler.

'The Story of Lahcen and Idir', 1967

At Beni Midar there is a barracks. It has many rows of small buildings, whitewashed, and everything is in the middle of big rocks, on the side of the mountain behind the town. A quiet place when the wind is not blowing. A few Spanish still live in the houses along the road. They run the shops. But now the people in the street are Moslems, mountain men with goats and sheep, or soldiers from the *cuartel* looking for wine. The Spanish sell wine to men they know. One Jew sells it to almost anybody. But there never is enough wine in the town for everybody who wants it. Beni Midar has only one street, that comes down out of the mountains, curves back and forth like a snake between the houses for a while, and goes on, back into the mountains. Sunday is a bad day, the one free time the soldiers have, when they can walk back and forth all day between the shops and houses. A few Spaniards in black clothes go into the church at the hour when the Rhmara ride their donkeys out of the *souk*. Later the Spaniards come out of the church and go home. Nothing else happens because all the shops are shut. There is nothing the soldiers can buy.

Driss had been stationed for eight months in Beni Midar. Because the *cabran* in charge of his unit had been a neighbour of his in Tetuan, he was not unhappy. The *cabran* had a friend with a motorcycle. Together they went each month to Tetuan. There the *cabran* always saw Driss's sister, who made a big bundle of food to send back to the barracks for him. She sent him chickens and cakes, cigarettes and figs, and always many hard-boiled eggs. He shared the eggs with two or three friends, and did not complain about being in Beni Midar.

Not even the brothels were open on Sunday. It was the day when everyone walked from one end of the town to the other, back and forth, many times. Sometimes Driss walked like this with his friends. Usually he took his gun and went down into the valley to hunt for hares. When he came back at twilight he stopped in a small café at the edge of the town and had a glass of tea and a few pipes of kif. If it had not been the only café he would never have gone into it. Shameful things happened there. Several times he had seen men from the mountains get up from the mat and do dances that left blood on the floor. These men were Djilala, and no one thought of stopping them, not even Driss. They did not dance because they wanted to dance, and it was this that made him angry and ashamed. It seemed to him that the world should be made in such a way that a man is free to dance or not as he feels. A Djilali can do only what the music tells him to do. When the musicians, who are Djilala too, play the music that has the power, his eyes shut and he falls on the floor. And until the man has shown the proof and tasted his own blood, the musicians do not begin the music that will bring him back to the world. They should do something about it, Driss said to the other soldiers who went with him to the café, and they agreed.

He had talked about it with his *cabran* in the public garden. The *cabran* said that when all the children in the land were going to school every day there would be no more *djenoun*. Women would no longer be able to put spells on their husbands. And the Djilala and the Hamatcha and all the others would stop cutting their legs and arms and chests. Driss thought about this for a long time. He was glad to hear that the government knew about these bad things. 'But if they know,' he thought, 'why don't they do something now? The day they get every one of the children in school I'll be lying beside Sidi Ali el Mandri.' He was thinking of the cemetery at Bab Sebta in Tetuan. When he saw the *cabran* again he said: 'If they can do something about it, they ought to do it now.' The *cabran* did not seem interested. 'Yes,' he said.

When Driss got his permission and went home he told his father what the *cabran* had said. 'You mean the government thinks it can kill all evil spirits?' his father cried.

'That's right. It can,' said Driss. 'It's going to.'

His father was old and had no confidence in the young men

who now ran the government. 'It's impossible,' he said. 'They should let them alone. Leave them under their stones. Children have gone to school before, and how many were hurt by *djenoun*? But if the government begins to make trouble for them, you'll see what will happen. They'll go after the children first.'

Driss had expected his father to speak this way, but when he heard the words he was ashamed. He did not answer. Some of his friends were without respect for God. They ate during Ramadan and argued with their fathers. He was glad not to be like them. But he felt that his father was wrong.

One hot summer Sunday when the sky was very blue Driss lay in bed late. The men who slept in his room at the barracks had gone out. He listened to the radio. 'It would be good down in the valley on a day like this,' he thought. He saw himself swimming in one of the big pools, and he thought of the hot sun on his back afterwards. He got up and unlocked the cupboard to look at his gun. Even before he took it out he said, '*Yah latif!*' because he remembered that he had only one cartridge left, and it was Sunday. He slammed the cupboard door shut and got back into bed. The radio began to give the news. He sat up, spat as far out as he could from the bed, and turned it off. In the silence he heard many birds singing in the *safsaf* tree outside the window. He scratched his head. Then he got up and dressed. In the court-yard he saw Mehdi going towards the stairs. Mehdi was on his way to do sentry duty in the box outside the main gate.

'*Khaï!* Does four rials sound good to you?'

Mehdi looked at him. 'Is this number sixty, three, fifty-one?' This was the name of an Egyptian song that came over the radio nearly every day. The song ended with the word nothing. Nothing, nothing, sung over and over again.

'Why not?' As they walked along together, Driss moved closer, so that his thigh rubbed against Mehdi's.

'The price is ten, *khoya*.'

'With all its cartridges?'

'You want me to open it up and show you here?' Mehdi's voice was angry. The words came out of the side of his mouth.

Driss said nothing. They came to the top of the stairs. Mehdi was walking fast. 'You'll have to have it back here by seven,' he said. 'Do you want it?'

In his head Driss saw the long day in the empty town. 'Yes,' he said. 'Stay there.' He hurried back to the room, unlocked his cupboard, and took out his gun. From the shelf he pulled down his pipe, his kif and a loaf of bread. He put his head outside the door. There was no one in the courtyard but Mehdi sitting on the wall at the other end. Then with the old gun in his hands he ran all the way to Mehdi. Mehdi took it and went down the stairs, leaving his own gun lying on the wall. Driss took up the gun, waited a moment, and followed him. When he went past the sentry box he heard Mehdi's voice say softly: 'I need the ten at seven, *khoya*.'

Driss grunted. He knew how dark it was in there. No officer ever stuck his head inside the door on Sundays. Ten rials, he thought, and he's running no risk. He looked around at the goats among the rocks. The sun was hot, but the air smelled sweet, and he was happy to be walking down the side of the mountain. He pulled the visor of his cap farther down over his eyes and began to whistle. Soon he came out in front of the town, below it on the other side of the valley. He could see the people on the benches in the park at the top of the cliff, small but clear and black. They were Spaniards and they were waiting for the bell of their church to begin to ring.

He got to the highest pool about the time the sun was overhead. When he lay on the rocks afterwards eating his bread, the sun burned him. No animals will move before three, he thought. He put his trousers on and crawled into the shade of the oleander bushes to sleep. When he awoke the air was cooler. He smoked all the kif he had, and went walking through the valley. Sometimes he sang. He found no hares, and so he put small stones on the tops of the rocks and fired at them. Then he climbed back up the other side of the valley and followed the highway into the town.

He came to the café and went in. The musicians were playing an *aaita* and singing. The tea drinkers clapped their hands with the music. A soldier cried: 'Driss! Sit down!' He sat with his

friends and smoked some of their kif. Then he bought four rials'
worth from the cutter who sat on the platform with the musicians,
and went on smoking. 'Nothing was moving in the valley today,'
he told them. 'It was dead down there.'

A man with a yellow turban on his head who sat nearby closed
his eyes and fell against the man next to him. The others around
him moved to a farther part of the mat. The man toppled over
and lay on the floor.

'Another one?' cried Driss. 'They should stay in Djebel Habib.
I can't look at him.'

The man took a long time to get to his feet. His arms and legs
had been captured by the drums, but his body was fighting, and
he groaned. Driss tried to pay no attention to him. He smoked
his pipe and looked at his friends, pretending that no Djilali was
in front of him. When the man pulled out his knife he could not
pretend any longer. He watched the blood running into the man's
eyes. It made a blank red curtain over each hole. The man opened
his eyes wider, as if he wanted to see through the blood. The
drums were loud.

Driss got up and paid the *qahouaji* for his tea. He said goodbye to the others and went out. The sun would soon go below
the top of the mountain. Its light made him want to shut his eyes,
because he had a lot of kif in his head. He walked through the
town to the higher end and turned into a lane that led up into
another valley. In this place there was no one. Cacti grew high
on each side of the lane, and the spiders had built a world of
webs between their thorns. Because he walked fast, the kif began
to boil in his head. Soon he was very hungry, but all the fruit
had been picked from the cacti along the lane. He came to a
small farmhouse with a thatched roof. Behind it on the empty
mountainside there were more cacti still pink with hundreds of
hindiyats. A dog in a shed beside the house began to bark. There
was no sign of people. He stood still for a while and listened to
the dog. Then he walked towards the cactus patch. He was sure
no one was in the house. Many years ago his sister had shown
him how to pick *hindiyats* without letting the needles get into
the flesh of his hands. He laid his gun on the ground behind a

low stone wall and began to gather the fruit. As he picked he
saw in his head the two blind red holes of the Djilali's eyes, and
under his breath he cursed all Djilala. When he had a great pile
of fruit on the ground he sat down and began to eat, throwing
the peels over his shoulder. As he ate he grew hungrier, and so
he picked more. The picture he had in his head of the man's face
shiny with blood slowly faded. He thought only of the *hindiyats*
he was eating. It was almost dark there on the mountainside. He
looked at his watch and jumped up, because he remembered that
Mehdi had to have his gun at seven o'clock. In the dim light he
could not see the gun anywhere. He searched behind the wall,
where he thought he had laid it, but saw only stones and bushes.

'It's gone, *Allah istir*,' he said. His heart pounded. He ran back
to the lane and stood there a while. The dog barked without
stopping.

It was dark before he reached the gate of the barracks. Another
man was in the sentry box. The *cabran* was waiting for him in
the room. The old gun Driss's father had given him lay on his
bed.

'Do you know where Mehdi is?' the *cabran* asked him.

'No,' said Driss.

'He's in the dark house, the son of a whore. And do you know
why?'

Driss sat down on the bed. The *cabran* is my friend, he was
thinking. 'It's gone,' he said, and told him how he had laid the
gun on the ground, and a dog had been barking, and no one had
come by, and still it had disappeared. 'Maybe the dog was a
djinn,' he said when he had finished. He did not really believe
the dog had anything to do with it, but he could not think of
anything else to say then.

The *cabran* looked at him a long time and said nothing. He
shook his head. 'I thought you had some brains,' he said at last.
Then his face grew very angry, and he pulled Driss out into the
courtyard and told a soldier to lock him up.

At ten o'clock that night he went to see Driss. He found him
smoking his *sebsi* in the dark. The cell was full of kif smoke.
'Garbage!' cried the *cabran*, and he took the pipe and the kif

away from him. 'Tell the truth,' he said to Driss. 'You sold the gun, didn't you?'

'On my mother's head, it's just as I told you! There was only the dog.'

The *cabran* could not make him say anything different. He slammed the door and went to the café in the town to have a glass of tea. He sat listening to the music, and he began to smoke the kif he had taken from Driss. If Driss was telling the truth, then it was only the kif in Driss's head that had made him lose the gun, and in that case there was a chance that it could be found.

The *cabran* had not smoked in a long time. As the kif filled his head he began to be hungry, and he remembered the times when he had been a boy smoking kif with his friends. Always they had gone to look for *hindiyats* afterwards, because they tasted better than anything else and cost nothing. They always knew where there were some growing. 'A *kouffa* full of good *hindiyats*,' he thought. He shut his eyes and went on thinking.

The next morning early the *cabran* went out and stood on a high rock behind the barracks, looking carefully all around the valley and the bare mountainside. Not far away he saw a lane with cacti along it, and farther up there was a whole forest of cactus. 'There,' he said to himself.

He walked among the rocks until he came to the lane, and he followed the lane to the farmhouse. The dog began to bark. A woman came to the doorway and looked at him. He paid no attention to her, but went straight to the high cacti on the hillside behind the house. There were many *hindiyats* still to be eaten, but the *cabran* did not eat any of them. He had no kif in his head and he was thinking only of the gun. Beside a stone wall there was a big pile of *hindiya* peelings. Someone had eaten a great many. Then he saw the sun shining on part of the gun's barrel under the peelings. 'Hah!' he shouted, and he seized the gun and wiped it all over with his handkerchief. On his way back to the barracks he felt so happy that he decided to play a joke on Driss.

He hid the gun under his bed. With a glass of tea and a piece of bread in his hand he went to see Driss. He found him asleep on the floor in the dark.

'Daylight is here!' he shouted. He laughed and kicked Driss's foot to wake him up. Driss sat on the floor drinking the tea and the *cabran* stood in the doorway scratching his chin. He looked down at the floor, but not at Driss. After a time he said: 'Last night you told me a dog was barking?'

Driss was certain the *cabran* was going to make fun of him. He was sorry he had mentioned the dog. 'Yes,' he said, not sounding sure.

'If it was the dog,' the *cabran* went on, 'I know how to get it back. You have to help me.'

Driss looked up at him. He could not believe the *cabran* was being serious. Finally he said in a low voice: 'I was joking when I said that. I had kif in my head.'

The *cabran* was angry. 'You think it's a joke to lose a gun that belongs to the Sultan? You did sell it! You haven't got kif in your head now. Maybe you can tell the truth.' He stepped towards Driss, and Driss thought he was going to hit him. He stood up quickly. 'I told you the truth,' he said. 'It was gone.'

The *cabran* rubbed his chin and looked down at the floor again for a minute. 'The next time a Djilali begins to dance in the café, we'll do it,' he told him. He shut the door and left Driss alone.

Two days later the *cabran* came again to the dark house. He had another soldier with him. 'Quick!' he told Driss. 'There's one dancing now.'

They went out into the courtyard and Driss blinked his eyes. 'Listen,' said the *cabran*. 'When the Djilali is drinking his own blood he has power. What you have to do is ask him to make the *djinn* bring me the gun. I'm going to sit in my room and burn *djaoui*. That may help.'

'I'll do it,' said Driss. 'But it won't do any good.'

The other soldier took Driss to the café. The Djilali was a tall man from the mountains. He had already taken out his knife, and he was waving it in the air. The soldier made Driss sit down near the musicians, and then he waited until the man began to lick the blood from his arms. Then, because he thought he might be sick if he watched any longer, Driss raised his right arm towards the Djilali and said in a low voice: 'In the name of Allah, *khoya*, make the *djinn* that stole Mehdi's gun take it now to Aziz the *cabran*.' The Djilali seemed to be staring at him, but Driss could not be sure whether he had heard his words or not.

The soldier took him back to the barracks. The *cabran* was sitting under a plum tree beside the kitchen door. He told the soldier to go away and jumped up. 'Come,' he said, and he led Driss to the room. The air was blue with the smoke of the *djaoui* he had been burning. He pointed to the middle of the floor. 'Look!' he cried. A gun was lying there. Driss ran and picked it up. After he had looked at it carefully, he said: 'It's the gun.' And his voice was full of fear. The *cabran* could see that Driss had not been sure the thing was possible, but that now he no longer had any doubt.

The *cabran* was happy to have fooled him so easily. He laughed. 'You see, it worked,' he said. 'It's lucky for you. Mehdi's going to be in the dark house for another week.'

Driss did not answer. He felt even worse than when he had been watching the Djilali slicing the flesh of his arms.

That night he lay in bed worrying. It was the first time he had had anything to do with a *djinn* or an *affrit*. Now he had entered into their world. It was a dangerous world and he did not trust the *cabran* any longer. 'What am I going to do?' he thought. The men all around him were sleeping, but he could not close his eyes. Soon he got up and stepped outside. The leaves of the *safsaf* tree were hissing in the wind. On the other side of the courtyard there was light in one of the windows. Some of the officers were talking there. He walked slowly around the garden in the middle and looked up at the sky, thinking of how different his life was going to be now. As he came near the lighted window he heard a great burst of laughter. The *cabran* was telling a story. Driss stopped walking and listened.

'And he said to the Djilali: "Please, sidi, would you ask the dog that stole my gun—"'

The men laughed again, and the sound covered the *cabran's* voice.

He went quickly back and got into bed. If they knew he had heard the *cabran's* story they would laugh even more. He lay in the bed thinking, and he felt poison come into his heart. It was the *cabran's* fault that the *djinn* had been called, and now in front of his superior officers he was pretending that he had nothing to do with it. Later the *cabran* came in and went to bed, and it was quiet in the courtyard, but Driss lay thinking for a long time before he went to sleep.

In the days that came after that, the *cabran* was friendly again, but Driss did not want to see him smile. He thought with hatred: 'In his head I'm afraid of him now because he knows how to call a *djinn*. He jokes with me now because he has power.'

He could not laugh or be happy when the *cabran* was nearby. Each night he lay awake for a long time after the others had gone to sleep. He listened to the wind moving the hard leaves of the *safsaf* tree, and he thought only of how he could break the *cabran's* power.

When Mehdi came out of the dark house he spoke against the *cabran*. Driss paid him his ten rials. 'A lot of money for ten days in the dark house,' Mehdi grumbled, and he looked at the bill in his hand. Driss pretended not to understand. 'He's a son of a whore,' he said.

Mehdi snorted. 'And you have the head of a needle,' he said. 'It all came from you. The wind blows the kif out of your ears!'

'You think I wasn't in the dark house too?' cried Driss. But he could not tell Mehdi about the Djilali and the dog. 'He's a son of a whore,' he said again.

Mehdi's eyes grew narrow and stiff. 'I'll do his work for him. He'll think he's in the dark house himself when I finish.'

Mehdi went on his way. Driss stood watching him go.

The next Sunday Driss got up early and walked into Beni Midar. The *souk* was full of rows of mountain people in white clothes. He walked in among the donkeys and climbed the steps to the stalls. There he went to see an old man who sold incense and herbs. People called him El Fqih. He sat down in front of El Fqih and said: 'I want something for a son of a whore.'

El Fqih looked at him angrily. 'A sin!' He raised his forefinger

and shook it back and forth. 'Sins are not my work.' Driss did
not say anything. El Fqih spoke more quietly now. 'To balance
that, it is said that each trouble in the world has its remedy. There
are cheap remedies and remedies that cost a lot of money.' He
stopped.

Driss waited. 'How much is this one?' he asked him. The old
man was not pleased because he wanted to talk longer. But he
said: 'I'll give you a name for five rials.' He looked sternly at
Driss, leaned forward and whispered a name in his ear. 'In the
alley behind the sawmill,' he said aloud. 'The blue tin shack with
the canebrake behind it.' Driss paid him and ran down the steps.

He found the house. The old woman stood in the doorway with
a checked tablecloth over her head. Her eyes had turned white
like milk. They looked to Driss like the eyes of an old dog. He
said: 'You're Anisa?'

'Come into the house,' she told him. It was almost dark inside.
He told her he wanted something to break the power of a son of
a whore. 'Give me ten rials now,' she said. 'Come back at sunset
with another ten. It will be ready.'

After the midday meal he went out into the courtyard. He met
Mehdi and asked him to go with him to the café in Beni Midar.
They walked through the town in the hot afternoon sun. It was
still early when they got to the café, and there was plenty of
space on the mats. They sat in a dark corner. Driss took out his
kif and his *sebsi* and they smoked. When the musicians began
to play, Mehdi said: 'The circus is back!' But Driss did not want
to talk about the Djilala. He talked about the *cabran*. He gave
the pipe many times to Mehdi, and he watched Mehdi growing
more angry with the *cabran* as he smoked. He was not surprised
when Mehdi cried: 'I'll finish it tonight!'

'No, *khoya*,' said Driss. 'You don't know. He's gone way up.
He's a friend of all the officers now. They bring him bottles of
wine.'

'He'll come down,' Mehdi said. 'Before dinner tonight. In the
courtyard. You be there and watch it.'

Driss handed him the pipe and paid for the tea. He left Mehdi
there and went into the street to walk up and down because he

did not want to sit still any longer. When the sky was red behind the mountain he went to the alley by the sawmill. The old woman was in the doorway.

'Come in,' she said as before. When they were inside the room she handed him a paper packet. 'He has to take all of it,' she said. She took the money and pulled at his sleeve. 'I never saw you,' she said. 'Goodbye.'

Driss went to his room and listened to the radio. When dinner time came he stood inside the doorway looking out into the courtyard. In the shadows at the other end he thought he could see Mehdi, but he was not sure. There were many soldiers walking around in the courtyard, waiting for dinner. Soon there was shouting near the top of the steps. The soldiers began to run towards the other end of the courtyard. Driss looked from the doorway and saw only the running soldiers. He called to the men in the room. 'Something's happening!' They all ran out. Then with the paper of powder in his hand he went back into the room to the *cabran's* bed and lifted up the bottle of wine one of the officers had given the *cabran* the day before. It was almost full. He pulled out the cork and let the powder slide into the bottle. He shook the bottle and put the cork back. There was still shouting in the courtyard. He ran out. When he got near the crowd, he saw Mehdi being dragged along the ground by three soldiers. He was kicking. The *cabran* sat on the wall with his head down, holding his arm. There was blood all over his face and shirt.

It was almost half an hour before the *cabran* came to eat his dinner. His face was covered with bruises and his arm was bandaged and hung in a sling. Mehdi had cut it with his knife at the last minute when the soldiers had begun to pull them apart. The *cabran* did not speak much, and the men did not try to talk with him. He sat on his bed and ate. While he was eating he drank all the wine in the bottle.

That night the *cabran* moaned in his sleep. A dry wind blew between the mountains. It made a great noise in the *safsaf* tree outside the window. The air roared and the leaves rattled, but Driss still heard the *cabran's* voice crying. In the morning the doctor came to look at him. The *cabran's* eyes were open but he could not see. And his mouth was open but he could not speak. They carried him out of the room where the soldiers lived and put him somewhere else. 'Maybe the power is broken now,' thought Driss.

A few days later a truck came to the barracks, and he saw two men carrying the *cabran* on a stretcher to the truck. Then he was sure that the *cabran's* soul had been torn out of his body and that the power was truly broken. In his head he made a prayer of thanks to Allah. He stood with some other soldiers on a rock above the barracks watching the truck grow smaller as it moved down the mountain.

'It's bad for me,' he told a man who stood nearby. 'He always brought me food from home.' The soldier shook his head.

MY KING

Henri Michaux

In France the tradition of drug usage for literary creativity has been as strong as anywhere in the Western hemisphere—the most famous names of recent years being Antonin Artaud, Jean Cocteau and Henri Michaux. Of these three Cocteau is the one most widely known, and his book Opium—The Diary of a Cure *is among the most impressive drug documents. Cocteau—poet, novelist, playwright, artist and film producer—was first introduced to the drug in the 1920s, when opium smoking became very fashionable in certain European circles. In 1924, when he was suffering from depression because of the death of his lover, Raymond Radiguet, he began to use the drug constantly and, by 1928, was so weak and ill that he needed treatment. The story of the ensuing winter and Cocteau's cure are brilliantly recounted in* Opium, *and he was later to utilise the experiences in another work,* Les Enfants Terribles, *which he also filmed. Artaud, the poet, was also a great enthusiast of the cinema and spent many years exploring its 'surrealistic possibilities'. His addiction to drugs spanned the larger part of his life; it was intensified after a visit to Mexico in 1936 and most of his remaining years were spent in a mental home seeking a cure. Many of his poems and some of his works, such as* Heliogabale, *are influenced by his visionary experiences. The third member of this triumvirate is the most important in the context of this book, for Henri Michaux (1899–1979) devoted much of his life to the study of drugs and wrote several of this century's most important works on the subject.*

A complex, retiring man who was rarely photographed during his life, Michaux spent much of his childhood in self-imposed isolation, buried in books on mysticism and travel, two of the major interests of his life. As a young man he lived for a brief period in Paris, where he met several painters—including Paul Klee and Max Ernst—and developed his own artistic style, and then took to the sea, visiting South America and the Far East. In Ecuador he had his first contact with drugs. 'He took opium, which disappointed him,' his biographer Malcolm Bowie tells us, 'and ether, which held him in momentary fascination.' The seeds of inquiry were sown, however, and on his return to Paris he began the systematic study of mescaline, ether and several other hallucinogens which occupied much of the rest of his life. The results and impressions of this study are to be found primarily in three of his books, Les Rêves et la Jambe, Ecuador *and* La Nuit Remue, *the last of which contains some of the finest writing published on ether as an aid to self-analysis. Commenting on his work, Bowie says, 'No non-scientific commentator on the hallucinogens has provided a greater variety of information than Michaux on the ways in which drugs may affect our manipulation of language. The excessive resources of language and the aptitudes of the language-user are dominant issues in his studies.'*

The story I have selected is taken from La Nuit Remue *which helped to establish him as one of the most original and important French writers since Baudelaire and Rimbaud, both of whom he resembled in some respects. His bizarre style caused certain critics to say that his work was not literature at all, but drug hallucination at its most uncontrolled. For me it is visionary writing in the fine tradition we have seen throughout the pages of this book. The drawings were made by Michaux under the influence of mescaline.*

*   *   *

Into the very spot of suffering and of obsession you introduce such exultation, such magnificent violence, together with the hammering of words, that the pain, gradually dissolving, is replaced by an ethereal and demoniacal ball—wonderful state!

Epreuves, Exorcismes, 1945

In my night I besiege my King, I rise up gradually and I wring his neck.

He recovers his strength, I go at him again, and wring his neck once more.

I shake him, and shake him like an old plumtree, and his crown totters on his head.

And yet he is my King, I know it and he knows it, and there's no doubt that I'm at his service.

But in the night the passion of my hands strangles him without respite. But nothing belowboard. I arrive bare-handed and I squeeze the King's neck.

And this is my King, whom I have vainly strangled for so long in the privacy of my little room; his face, first bluish, after a short while looks natural, and his head bobs up again each night, each night.

In the privacy of my little room, I fart at the King's face. Then I burst out laughing. He tries to maintain a serene countenance, with all sense of insult wiped clean. But I fart at his face without stopping except to turn round towards him and burst out laughing in his noble face, which tries to retain some of its majesty.

Thus I conduct myself with him; beginning without end of my obscure life.

And now I dump him on the ground, and sit down on his face—his august face disappears from sight—my dirty old trousers with their oil stains, and my behind—for this, after all, is what it's called—straddle without embarrassment the face which was made for ruling.

And I make no bones about turning to left and right, oh no, when I feel like it or even more often, without caring whether his eyes or his nose are in the way. I go away only when I'm tired of sitting.

And if I look back, his imperturbable face reigns, always.

I slap him, I slap him, then in mockery I wipe his nose like a child's.

But it's perfectly clear that it is he who is King, and I his subject, his only subject.

Kicking him in the arse I drive him out of my room. I cover

him with garbage and dirt. I break plates on his legs. I ram
his ears with low and pertinent insults to hurt him deeply and
shamefully, with Neapolitan slanders so nasty and circumstantial
that one alone is a stain impossible to eradicate—some base suit
made to measure: the very stale of existence.

Well, I have to start all over again next day.

He has returned; he is there. He is always there. He can't clear
out for good. He absolutely must impose his damnable royal
presence on me in my room which is already too small.

It too often happens that I am involved in lawsuits. I contract
debts, I fight with knives, I do violence to children, I can't help
it, I don't succeed in penetrating myself with the spirit of the
Laws.

When my opponent has laid bare his grievances before the
court, my King, hardly listening to my excuses, recapitulates my
opponent's case, and it becomes in his august mouth the speech
of the public prosecutor, the terrible preliminary of the judgement
which is about to fall upon me.

Only at the end does he bring up a few useless quibbles.

The opponent, judging that these don't matter, prefers to withdraw these few subsidiary complaints which the court disregards. He is satisfied merely to be assured of the rest.

Just at this moment my King recapitulates the argument again from the beginning, always as if he were doing it on his own behalf, but pruning it slightly. Having done this and established agreement on points of detail, he once more resumes the argument from the beginning, and, weakening it little by little, step by step, stage by stage, he reduces it to such balderdash that the humiliated court and the magistrates in full conclave wonder how anyone has dared to convene them for such trifles, and a negative judgement is returned in the midst of the hilarity and jeers of the spectators.

Then my King, without bothering about me, as if I had nothing to do with it, gets up and goes off, impenetrable.

It may be asked whether this is a job for a King; it's there, though, that he shows what he is, this tyrant, who can do nothing, can let nothing be done without showing his spellbinding power that crushes and leaves no recourse.

What an imbecile I was, trying to put him outdoors! Why not have calmly left him in my room, calmly without bothering about him.

But no. Imbecile that I was, and he, seeing how easy it was to reign, will soon tyrannise over a whole country.

Wherever he goes, he installs himself.

And nobody is astonished, it seems as if his place had always been there.

One waits, one doesn't speak a word, one waits for Him to decide.

In my little room animals come and go. Not at the same time. Not intact. But they pass through, a shabby retinue that mocks the forms of nature. The lion enters with head low, puckered, and bruised like an old clothes bag. His poor old paws waver along. He progresses somehow or other, like some poor wretch.

The elephant comes in deflated and less solid than a fawn.

So with the rest of the animals.

No machinery. No engines. The automobile comes in utterly flattened out and as a last resort could serve as a floor.

Such is my little room where my inflexible King wishes nothing, except what he has mistreated, confounded, reduced to nothing, where I however have summoned so many creatures to be my companions.

Even the rhinoceros, that brute which cannot bear man, which rushes on everything (and so solid, hewn like a boulder), the rhinoceros himself one day came in a fog, almost impalpable, evasive and unresisting . . . and wavered along.

A hundred times stronger than he was the little curtain of the skylight, a hundred times stronger than he, the strong and impetuous rhinoceros which recoils before nothing.

But my King doesn't want rhinoceroses to come in unless they are feeble and dripping away.

Another time maybe he will permit him to move round on crutches . . . and, to keep him in bounds, a pretence of skin, a tender childlike skin which a grain of sand would tear off.

This is the way that my King authorises the animals to pass before us. This way only.

He reigns; he has me; he doesn't care for diversions.

This little hand, so stiff in my pocket, is all that remains to me of my fiancée.

A dry and mummified little hand (can it really have belonged to her?). It is all he has left me of Her.

He has ravished her from me. He has corrupted her away from me. He has reduced her to nothing for me!

In my little room the palace sessions are of all things the most miserable.

Even the serpents are not low enough, nor cringing enough for him, even a motionless pine tree would affront him.

Then too, what appears at his Court (at our poor little room!) is so incredibly disappointing that the lowest of proletarians would not long for it.

Besides, who but my King, and I who am used to it, could

trap a respectful creature into these advances and recoils of dim nature, these little frolics of dead leaves, these thinly scattered drops which fall, heavy and desolate, into silence.

Vain homage anyway!

Imperceptible are the movements of his face, imperceptible.

THE BLOOD OF A WIG

Terry Southern

Probably best known as the author of Candy, *one of the most notorious sex novels of the Sixties, Terry Southern (1924–1995) also possessed a wide knowledge of drugs and drug literature which left its mark on many of his essays, short stories and novels, among them* The Magic Christian *(1959) and* Blue Movie *(1970). Indeed, the present book owes much to his expertise, for I first discussed the idea with him in New York in 1966, while we were both involved in the publication of the first unexpurgated British edition of* Candy. *As a result of our conversation, several of the pieces I included had his enthusiastic approval.*

Born in Texas, the son of a pharmacist, Southern's literary career began in his teens when he started rewriting Poe's most bizarre, stimulant-inspired stories which he believed 'had not gone far enough'. After service during the Second World War, he went for a time to Paris where he lived in 'a miasma of hashish and Arab Quarter bepop' while progressing from outrageous short stories to on-the-edge novels and brilliantly idiosyncratic screenplays. His novel Candy *was written in 1958 for the Olympia Press in Paris, and did not appear under his own name in the United States until 1964.*

Back in America and living in Greenwich Village, Southern began an association with Stanley Kubrick and wrote the scripts for some now legendary movies, among them Dr Strangelove *(1964),* Barbarella *(1967) and* Easy Rider *(1968). Sadly, the film version of* Candy *(1968) failed to capture the spirit of this Voltaire-inspired novel about a randy sexual innocent, but his reputation was already assured and he was one of the faces immortalised on the sleeve of the Beatles' classic album,* Sergeant Pepper's Lonely Hearts Club Band.

Some of the most revealing insights into Terry Southern's experiences with drugs are to be found in the stories 'Red Dirt Marijuana', written for Evergreen Review *in 1964 and subsequently the title story for a collection of his work issued in 1967, and 'The Blood of a Wig' which I am including here. This darkly satirical story of drug-taking among the 'ten-to-four Mad Ave. crowd' of New York is typical of its time and the attitude of 'smart' Americans—and their European counterparts, for that matter—towards stimulants and hallucinogens. William Burroughs, with whom he invented a potion called 'Brompton's Mixture' (a combination of alcohol, cocaine, morphine and cherry syrup), called the story 'one of the bizarrest I have ever read . . . and what with all this moving of hearts and brains from one place to another, it could happen anywhere.'*

*   *   *

How come it's against the law if it's so all-fired good?' asked Harold . . . 'I tell you what it is,' he said then, 'it's 'cause a man see too much when he get high, that's what. He see right through everything . . . a man get high, he sees right through all them tricks, an' lies, and all that old bull-crap. He see right through into the truth of it all.'

'Red Dirt Marijuana', 1967

My most outlandish drug experience, now that I think about it, didn't occur with beat Village or Harlem weirdos, but during a brief run with the ten-to-four Mad Ave. crowd.

How it happened, this friend of mine who was working at *Lance* ('The Mag for Men') phoned me one morning—he knew I was strapped.

'One of the fiction editors is out with syph or something,' he said. 'You want to take his place for a while?'

I was still mostly asleep, so I tried to cool it by shooting a few incisive queries as to the nature of the gig—which he couldn't seem to follow.

'Well,' he said finally, 'you won't have to *do* anything, if that's what you mean.' He had a sort of blunt and sullen way about him—John Fox his name was, an ex-Yalie and would-be writer who was constantly having to 'put it back on the shelf,' as he expressed it (blunt, sullen), and take one of these hot-shot Mad Ave, jobs, and always for some odd reason—like at present, paying for his mom's analysis.

Anyway, I accepted the post, and now I had been working there about three weeks. It wasn't true, of course, what he'd said about not having to do anything—I mean the way he had talked I wouldn't even have to get out of bed—but after three weeks my routine was fairly smooth: up at ten, wash face, brush teeth, fresh shirt, dex, and make it. I had this transistor-shaver I'd copped for five off a junky-booster, so I would shave with it in the cab, and walk into the office at ten-thirty or so, dapper as Dan and hip as Harry. Then into my own small office, lock the door, and start stashing the return-postage from the unsolicited mss. We would get an incredible amount of mss—about two hundred a day—and these were divided into two categories: (1) those from agents, and (2) those that came in cold, straight from the author. The ratio was about 30 to 1 in favour of the latter— which formed a gigantic heap called 'the shit-pile', or (by the girl-readers) 'the garbage dump'. These always contained a lot of return-postage—so right away I was able to supplement my weekly wage by seven or eight dollars a day in postage stamps. Everyone else considered the 'shit-pile' as something heinously repugnant, especially the sensitive girl ('garbage') readers, so it was a source of irritation and chagrin to my secretary when I first told her I wished to read 'all unsolicited manuscripts and no manuscripts from agents'.

John Fox found it incomprehensible.

'You must be out of your nut!' he said. 'Ha! Wait until you try to read some of that crap in the shit-pile!'

I explained however (and it was actually true in the beginning) that I had this theory about the existence of a *pure, primitive, folk-like* literature—which, if it did exist, could only turn up among the unsolicited mss. Or *weird*, something really *weird*, even insane, might turn up there—whereas I knew the stuff from the agents would be the same old predictably competent tripe. So, aside from stashing the stamps, I would read each of these shit-pile mss very carefully—reading subtleties, insinuations, multi-level entendre into what was actually just a sort of flat, straightforward simple-mindedness. I would think each was a put-on—a fresh and curious parody of some kind, and I would read on, and on, all the way to the end, waiting for the pay-off . . . but, of course, that never happened, and I gradually began to revise my theory and to refine my method. By the second week, I was able to reject an ms after reading the opening sentence, and by the third I could often reject on the basis of *title* alone—the principle being if an author would allow a blatantly dumbbell title, he was incapable of writing a story worth reading. (This was thoroughly tested and proved before adopting.) Then, instead of actually *reading* mss, I would spend hours, days really, just thinking, trying to refine and extend my method of blitz-rejection. I was able to take it a little farther, but not much. For example, any woman author who used 'Mrs' in her name could be rejected out of hand—*unless* it was used with only one name, like 'by Mrs Carter', then it might be a weirdie. And again, any author using a middle initial or a 'Jr' in his name, shoot it right back to him! I knew I was taking a chance with that one (because of Connell and Selby), but I figured what the hell, I could hardly afford to gear the sort of fast-moving synchro-mesh operation I had in mind to a couple of exceptions—which, after all, only went to prove the consarn rule, so to speak. Anyway, there it was, the end of the third week and the old job going smoothly enough, except that I had developed quite a little dexie habit by then—not actually a habit, of course, but a sort of very real dependence . . . having by nature a nocturnal metabolism whereby my day (pre-*Lance*) would ordinarily begin at three or four in the afternoon and finish at eight or nine in the morning. As a top-staffer at *Lance*, however, I had to make other arrangements. Early on I had actually asked John Fox if it would be possible for me to come in at four and work until midnight.

  'Are you out of your *nut*?' (That was his standard comeback.) 'Don't you know what's happening here? This is a *social* scene, man—these guys want to *see* you, they want to get to *know* you?'

'What are they, faggots?'

'No, they're not *faggots*,' he said stoutly, but then seemed hard pressed to explain, and shrugged it off. 'It's just that they don't have very much, you know, *to do*.'

It was true in a way that no one seemed to actually *do* anything—except for the typists, of course, always typing away. But the guys just sort of hung out, or around, buzzing each other, sounding the chicks, that sort of thing.

The point is though that I had to make it in by ten, or thereabouts. One reason for this was the 'pre-lunch confab' which Hacker, or the 'Old Man' (as, sure enough, the publisher was called) might decide to have on any given day. And so it came to pass that on this particular—Monday it was—morning, up promptly at nine-three-oh, wash face, brush teeth, fresh shirt, all as per usual, and reach for the dex . . . no dex, out of dex. This was especially inopportune because it was on top of two straight white and active nights, and it was somewhat as though an eight-hundred-pound bag of loosely packed sand began to settle slowly on the head. No panic, just immediate death from fatigue.

At Sheridan Square, where I usually got the taxi, I went into the drug store. The first-shift pharmacist, naturally a guy I had never seen before, was on duty. He looked like an ageing efficiency expert.

'Uh, I'd like to get some dexamyl, please.'

The pharmacist didn't say anything, just raised one hand to adjust his steel-rimmed glasses, and put the other out for the prescription.

'It's on file here,' I said, nodding towards the back.

'What name?' he wanted to know, then disappeared behind the glass partition, but very briefly indeed.

'Nope,' he said, coming back, and was already looking over my shoulder to the next customer.

'Could you call Mr Robbins?' I asked. 'He can tell you about it.' Of course this was simply whistling in the dark, since I was

pretty sure Robbins, the night-shift man, didn't know me by
name, but I had to keep the ball rolling.

'I'm not gonna wake Robbins at this hour—he'd blow his
stack. Who's next?'

'Well, listen, can't you just *give* me a couple—I've, uh, got a
long drive ahead.'

'You can't get dexies without a script,' he said, rather reproach-
fully, wrapping a box of Tampax for a teenie-bopper nifty behind
me, '*you* know that.'

'Okay, how about if I get the doctor to phone you?'

'Phone's up front,' he said, and to the nifty: 'That's
seventy-nine.'

The phone was under siege—one person using it, and about
five waiting—all, for some weird reason, spade fags and prancing
gay. Not that I give a damn about who uses the phone, it was just
one of those absurd incongruities that seem so often to conspire to
undo sanity in times of crisis. What the hell was going on? They
were obviously together, very excited, chattering like magpies.
Was it the Katherine Dunham contingent of male dancers?
Stranded? Lost? Why out so early? One guy had a list of numbers
in his hand the size of a small flag. I stood there for a moment,
confused in pointless speculation, then left abruptly and hurried
down West 4th to the dinette. This was doubly to purpose, since
not only is there a phone, but the place is frequented by all
manner of heads, and a casual score might well be in order—
though it *was* a bit early for the latter, granted.

And this did, in fact, prove to be the case. There was no one
there whom I knew—and, worse still, halfway to the phone, I
suddenly remembered my so-called doctor (Dr Friedman, his
name was) had gone to California on vacation a few days ago.
Christ almighty! I sat down at the counter. This called for a quick
think-through. Should I actually call him in California? Have him
phone the drugstore from there? Quite a production for a couple
of dex. I looked at my watch, it was just after seven in Los
Angeles—Friedman would blow his stack. I decided to hell with
it and ordered a cup of coffee. Then a remarkable thing happened.
I had sat down next to a young man who now quite casually

removed a small transparent silo-shaped vial from his pocket, and without so much as a glance in any direction, calmly tapped a couple of the belovedly familiar green-hearted darlings into his cupped hand, and tossed them off like two salted peanuts.

Deus ex machina!

'Uh, excuse me,' I said, in the friendliest sort of way, 'I just happened to notice you taking a couple of, ha, ha, dexamyl.' And I proceeded to lay my story on him—while he, after one brief look of appraisal, sat listening, his eyes straight ahead, hands still on the counter, one of them half covering the magic vial. Finally he just nodded and shook out two more on the counter. 'Have a ball,' he said.

I reached the office about five minutes late for the big pre-lunch confab. John Fox made a face of mild disgust when I came in the conference room. He always seemed to consider my flaws as his responsibility since it was he had recommended me for the post. Now he glanced uneasily at old Hacker, who was the publisher, editor-in-chief, etc., etc. A man of about fifty-five, he bore a striking resemblance to Edward G. Robinson—an image to which he gave further credence by frequently sitting in a squat-like manner, chewing an unlit cigar butt, and mouthing coarse expressions. He liked to characterise himself as a 'tough old bastard', one of his favourite prefaces being: 'I know most of you guys think I'm a *tough old bastard*, right? Well, maybe I am. In the quality-Lit game you *gotta* be tough!' And bla-bla-bla.

Anyway as I took my usual seat between Fox and Bert Katz, the feature-editor, old Hack looked at his watch, then back at me.

'Sorry,' I mumbled.

'We're running a *magazine* here, young man, not a *whorehouse*.'

'Right and double right,' I parried crisply. Somehow old Hack always brought out the schoolboy in me.

'If you want to be *late*,' he continued, 'be late at the *whorehouse*—and do it on your own time!'

Part of his design in remarks of this sort was to get a reaction from the two girls present—Maxine, his cutie pie private sec, and Miss Rogers, assistant to the Art Director—both of whom managed, as usual, a polite blush and half-lowered eyes for his benefit.

The next ten minutes were spent talking about whether to send our own exclusive third-rate photographer to Vietnam or to use the rejects of a second-rate one who had just come back.

'Even with the rejects we could still run our *E.L. trade*,' said Katz, referring to an italicised phrase 'Exclusively Lance' which appeared under photographs and meant they were not being published elsewhere—though less through exclusivity, in my view, than general crappiness.

Without really resolving this, we went on to the subject of Twiggy, the British fashion-model who had just arrived in New York and about whose boyish hair and bust-line raged a storm of controversy. What did it mean philosophically? Aesthetically? Did it signal a new trend? Should we adjust our centre-spread requirements (traditionally 42–24–38) to meet current taste? Or was it simply a flash fad?

'Come next issue,' said Hack, 'we don't want to find ourselves holding the wrong end of the shit-stick, now do we?'

Everyone was quick to agree.

'Well, *I* think she's absolutely *delightful*,' exclaimed Ronnie Rondell, the art director (prancing gay and proud of it), 'she's so much more . . . sensitive-looking and . . . *delicate* than those awful . . . *milk factories*!' He gave a little shiver of revulsion and looked around excitedly for corroboration.

Hack, who had a deep-rooted anti-fag streak, stared at him for a moment like he was some kind of weird lizard, and he seemed about to say something cruel and uncalled for to Ron, but then he suddenly turned on me instead.

'Well, Mister Whorehouse man, isn't it about time we heard from you? Got any ideas that might conceivably keep this operation out of the shit-house for another issue or two?'

'Yeah, well I've been thinking,' I said, winging it completely, 'I mean, Fox here and I had an idea for a series of interviews with unusual persons . . .'

'Unusual *persons*?' he growled, 'what the hell does that mean?'

'Well, you know, a whole new department, like a regular feature. Maybe call it, uh, "Lance Visits . . ."'

He was scowling, but he was also nodding vigorously. ' "Lance Visits . . ." Yeh, yeh, you wantta gimme a fer instance?'

'Well, you know, like, uh . . . "Lance Visits a Typical Teenie-Bopper"—cute teenie-bopper tells about cute teen-use of Sarah Wrap as a contraceptive, et cetera . . . and uh, let's see . . . "Lance Visits A Giant Spade Commie Bull Dike" . . . "Lance Visits the Author of *Masturbation Now!*", a really fun-guy'.

Now that I was getting warmed up, I was aware that Fox, on my left, had raised a hand to his face and was slowly massaging it, mouth open, eyes closed. I didn't look at Hack, but I knew he had stopped nodding. I pressed on . . . 'you see, it could become a sort of regular department, we could do a "*E. L.*" on it . . . "*Another Exclusive Lance Visit*". How about this one: "Lance Visits A Cute Junkie Hooker" . . . "Lance Visits A Zany Ex-Nun Nympho" . . . "Lance Visits the Fabulous Rose Chan, beautiful research and development technician for the so-called French Tickler" . . .'

'Okay,' said Hack, 'how about *this* one: "Lance Visits Lance"—know where? Up shit-creek without a paddle! Because that's where we'd be if we tried any of that stuff.' He shook his head in a lament of disgust and pity. 'Jez, that's some sense of humour you got, boy.' Then he turned to Fox. 'What rock you say you found him under? Jez.'

Fox, as per usual, made no discernible effort to defend me, simply pretended to suppress a yawn, eyes averted, continuing to doodle on his 'Think Pad', one of which lay by each of our ashtrays.

'Okay,' said Hack, lighting a new cigar, 'suppose *I* come up with an idea? I mean, I don't wantta *surprise* you guys, cause any *heart–attacks* . . . by *me* coming up with an *idea*,' he saying this with a benign serpent smile, then adding in grim significance, '*after twenty-seven years in this goddam game!*' He took a sip of water, as though trying to cool his irritation at being (as per usual) 'the only slob around here who delivers'. 'Now let's just stoke this one for a while,' he said, 'and see if it gets stiff. Okay, lemme ask you a question: what's the hottest thing in mags at this time? What's raising all the stink and hullabaloo? The *Manchester* book, right? The suppressed passages, right?' He was referring, of course, to a highly publicised account of the assassination of President Kennedy—certain passages of which had allegedly been deleted. 'Okay, now all this stink and hulla-baloo—*I* don't like it, *you* don't like it. In the first place, it's infringement on freedom of the press. In the second, they've exaggerated it all out of proportion. I mean, what the hell was *in* those passages? See what I mean? All right, suppose we do a *take-off* on those same passages?'

He gave me a slow look, eyes narrowed—ostensibly to protect them from his cigar smoke, but with a Mephistophelean effect. *He* knew that *I* knew that his 'idea' was actually an idea I had gotten from Paul Krassner, editor of *The Realist*, a few evenings earlier, and had mentioned, *en passant* so to speak, at the last pre-lunch confab. He seemed to be wondering if I would crack. A test, like. I avoided his eyes, doodled on the 'Think Pad'. He exhaled in my direction, and continued:

'Know what I mean? Something *light*, something *zany*, kid the pants off the guys who suppressed it in the first place. A satire like. Get the slant?'

No one at the table seemed to. Except for Hack we were all in our thirties or early forties, and each had been hurt in some way by the President's death. It was not easy to imagine any particular 'zaniness' in that regard.

Fox was the first to speak, somewhat painfully it seemed. 'I'm, uh, not quite sure I follow,' he said. 'You mean it would be done in the style of the book?'

'Right,' said Hack, 'but get this, we don't say it *is* the real thing, we say it *purports* to be the real thing. And editorially we *challenge* the *authenticity* of it! Am I getting through to you?'

'Well, uh, yeah,' said Fox, 'but I'm not sure it can be, you know, uh, *funny*.'

Hack shrugged. 'So? *You're* not sure, *I'm* not sure. Nobody's sure it can be funny. We all take a crack at it—just stroke it a while and see if we get any jissom—right?'

Right.

After work that evening I picked up a new dexamyl prescription and stopped off at Sheridan Square to get it filled. Coming out of the drug store, I paused momentarily to take in the scene. It was a fantastic evening—late spring evening, warm breeze promise of great summer evenings imminent—and teenies in minis floating by like ballerinas, young thighs flashing. Summer, I thought, will be the acid test for minis when it gets too warm for tights, body-stockings, that sort of thing. It should be quite an interesting phenomenon. On a surge of sex-dope impulse I decided to fall by the dinette and see if anything of special import was shaking, so to speak.

Curious that the first person I should see there, hunched over his coffee, frozen saintlike, black shades around his head as though a hippy crown of thorns, should be the young man who had given me the dex that very morning. I had the feeling he hadn't moved all day. But this wasn't true because he now had on a white linen suit and was sitting in a booth. He nodded in that brief formal way it is possible to nod and mean more than just hello. I sat down opposite him.

'I see you got yourself all straightened out,' he said with a wan smile, nodding again, this time at my little paper bag with the pharmacy label on it.

I took out the vial of dex and popped a quick one, thinking to do a bit of the old creative Lit later on. Then I shook out four or five and gave them to the young man. 'Here's some interest.'

'Any time,' he said, dropping them in his top pocket, and after a pause. 'You ever in the mood for something beside dexies?'

'Like what?'

He shrugged, 'Oh, you know,' he said, raising a vague limp hand, then added with a smile, 'I mean you know your moods better than I do.'

During the next five minutes he proved to be the most acquisitive pusher, despite his tender years, I have ever encountered.

His range was extensive—beginning with New Jersey pot, and ending with something called a 'Frisco Speedball', a concoction of heroin and cocaine, with a touch of acid ('gives it a little colour'). While we were sitting there, a veritable parade of his far-flung connections commenced, sauntering over, or past the booth, pausing just long enough to inquire if he wanted to score— for sleepers, leapers, creepers . . . acid in cubes, vials, capsules, tablets, powder . . . 'hash, baby, it's black as O' . . . mushrooms, mescaline, buttons . . . cosanyl, codeine, coke . . . coke in crystals, coke in powder, coke that looked like karo syrup . . . red birds, yellow jackets, purple hearts . . . 'liquid—O, man, it comes straight from Indo-China, stamped right on the can' . . . and from time to time the young man ('Trick' he was called) would turn to me and say: 'Got eyes?'

After committing to a modest (thirty dollars) score for crystals, and again for two ounces of what was purported to be 'Panamanian Green' ('It's "one-poke pot", baby.') I declined further inducement. At one point an extremely down-and-out type, a guy I had known before whose actual name was Rattman, but who was known with simple familiarity as 'Rat', and even more familiarly, though somehow obscurely, as 'The Rat-Prick Man', half staggered past the booth, clocked the acquisitive Trick, paused, moved uncertainly towards the booth, took a crumpled brown paper bag out of his coat pocket, and opened it to show.

'Trick,' he muttered, almost without moving his lips. '. . . Trick, can you use any Lights? Two-bits for the bunch.' We both looked in, on some commodity quite unrecognisable—tiny, dark cylinder-shaped capsules, brown-black with sticky guk, flat on each end, and apparently made of plastic. There was about a handful of them. The young man made a weary face of distaste and annoyance.

'Man,' he asked softly, plaintively, looking up at Rattman, '*when* are you going to get buried?'

But the latter, impervious, gave a soundless guffaw, and shuffled on.

'What,' I wanted to know, 'were those things?' asking this of the young man half in genuine interest, half in annoyance at not knowing. He shrugged, raised a vague wave of dismissal. 'Lights they're called . . . they're used nicotine filters. You know, those nicotine filters you put in a certain kind of cigarette holder.'

'*Used* nicotine filters? What do you do with them?'

'Well, you know, drop two or three in a cup of coffee—gives you a little buzz.'

'A little *buzz*?' I said, 'are you kidding? How about a little *cancer*? That's all tar and nicotine in there, isn't it?'

'Yeah, well, you know . . .' he chuckled dryly, 'anything for kicks. Right?'

Right, right, right.

And it was just about then he sprung it—first giving me his look of odd appraisal, then the sign, the tired smile, the halting deference: 'Listen, man . . . you ever made Red-Split?'

'I beg your pardon?'

'Yeah, you know—*the blood of a wig.*'

'No,' I said, not really understanding, 'I don't believe I have.'

'Well, it's something else, baby, I can tell you that.'

'Uh, well, *what* did you call it—I'm not sure I understood . . .'

' "Red-Split," man, it's called "Red-Split"—it's schizo-juice . . . *blood* . . . the blood of a wig.'

'Oh, I see.' I had, in fact, read about it in a recent article in the *Times*—how they had shot up a bunch of volunteer prisoners (very normal, healthy guys, of course) with the blood of schizophrenia patients—and the effect had been quite pronounced . . . in some cases, manic; in other cases, depressive—about 50/50 as I recalled.

'But that can be a big bring-down, can't it?'

He shook his head sombrely. 'Not with *this* juice it can't. You know who this is out of?' Then he revealed the source—Chin Lee, it was, a famous East Village resident, a Chinese symbolist poet, who was presently residing at Bellevue in a strait jacket. 'Nobody,' he said, 'and I mean *nobody*, baby, has gone anywhere but *up, up, up* on *this* taste!'

I thought that it might be an interesting experience, but using caution as my watchword (the *Times* article had been very sketchy) I had to know more about this so-called Red-Split, Blood of a Wig. 'Well, how long does it, uh, you know, *last*?'

He seemed a little vague about that—almost to the point of resenting the question. 'It's a *trip*, man—four hours, six if you're lucky. It all depends. It's a question of *combination*—how your blood makes it with his, you dig?' He paused and gave me a very straight look. 'I'll tell you this much, baby, it *cuts acid and STP* . . .' He nodded vigorously. 'That's right, cuts them both. *Back, down*, and *sideways*.'

'Really?'

He must have felt he was getting a bit too loquacious, a bit too much on the old hard-sell side, because then he just cooled it, and nodded. 'That's right,' he said, so soft and serious that it wasn't really audible.

'How much?' I asked, finally, uncertain of any other approach.

'I'll level with you,' he said, 'I've got this connection—a ward-attendant . . . you know, a male-nurse . . . has what you might call *access* to the hospital pharmacy . . . does a little trading with the guards on the fifth floor—that's where the *monstro*-wigs are—''High Five'' it's called. That's where Chin Lee's at. Anyway, he's operating at cost right now—I mean, he'll cop as much M, or whatever other hard-shit he can, from the pharmacy, then he'll go up to High Five and trade for the juice—you know, just fresh, straight, uncut wig-juice—90 cc., that's the regular hit, about an ounce, I guess . . . I mean, that's what they hit the wigs for, a 90 cc. syringe-full, then they cap the spike and put the whole outfit in an insulated wrapper. Like it's supposed to stay at body-temperature, you dig? They're very strict about that—about how much they tap the wig for, and about keeping it fresh and warm, that sort of thing. Which is okay, because that's the trip—90 cc., ''piping hot'', as they say.' He gave a tired little laugh at the curious image. 'Anyway the point is, he never knows in front what the *price* will be, my friend doesn't, because he never knows what kind of M score he'll make. I mean like if he scores for half-a-bill of M, then that's what he charges for the Split, you dig?'

To me, with my Mad Ave. savvy, this seemed fairly illogical.

'Can't he hold out on the High Five guys?' I asked, '. . . you know, tell them he only got half what he really got, and save it for later.'

He shrugged, almost unhappily. 'He's a very ethical guy,' he said, 'I mean like he's pretty weird. He's not really interested in narcotics, just *changes*. I mean, like he lets *them* do the count on the M—they tell him how much it's worth and that's what he charges for the Split.'

'That *is* weird,' I agreed.

'Yeah, well it's like a new market, you know. I mean there's no established price yet, he's trying to develop a clientele—can you make half-a-bill?'

While I pondered, he smiled his brave tired smile, and said: 'There's one thing about the cat, being so ethical and all—he'll never burn you.'

So in the end it was agreed, and he went off to complete the arrangements.

The effect of Red-Split was 'as advertised' so to speak—in this case, quite gleeful. Sense-derangement-wise it was unlike acid in that it was not a question of the *'Essential I'* having new insights, but of becoming a different person entirely. So that in a way there was nothing very scary about it, just extremely weird, and, as it turned out, somewhat mischievous (Chin Lee, incidentally, was not merely a great wig, but also a great wag). At about six in the morning I started to work on the alleged 'Manchester passages'. Krassner might be cross, I thought, but what the hell, you can't copyright an idea. Also I intended to give him full and ample credit. 'Darn good exposure for Paul,' I mused benignly, taking up the old magic quill.

The first few passages were fairly innocuous, the emphasis being on a style identical to that of the work in question. Towards the end of Chapter Six, however, I really started cooking: '. . . wan, and wholly bereft, she steals away from the others, moving trance-like towards the darkened rear-compartment where the casket rests. She enters, and a whispery circle of light shrouds her bowed head as she closes the door behind her and leans against it. Slowly she raises her eyes and takes a solemn step forward. She gasps, and is literally slammed back against the door by the sheer impact of the outrageous horror confronting her: i.e., the hulking Texan silhouette at the casket, its lid half raised, and he hunching bestially, his coarse animal member thrusting into the casket, and indeed into the neck-wound itself.

'*Great God,*' she cries, 'how heinous! It must be a case of . . . of . . . *NECK*-ROPHILIA!'' '

I finished at about ten, dexed, and made it to the office. I went directly into Fox's cubicle (the 'Lair' it was called).

'You know,' I began, lending the inflection a child-like candour, 'I could be wrong but I think I've *got* it,' and I handed him the ms.

'Got what?' he countered dryly, 'the clap?'

'You know, that Manchester thing we discussed at the last pre-lunch confab.' While he read, I paced about, flapped my arms in a gesture of uncertainty and humble doubt. 'Oh, it may need a little tightening up, brightening up, granted, but I hope you'll agree that the *essence* is there.'

For a while he didn't speak, just sat with his head resting on one hand staring down at the last page. Finally he raised his eyes; his eyes were always somehow sad.

'You really *are* out of your nut, aren't you?'

'Sorry, John,' I said, 'don't follow.'

He looked back at the ms, moved his hands a little away from it as though it were a poisonous thing. Then he spoke with great seriousness:

'I think you ought to have your head examined.'

'My *head* is swell,' I said, and wished to elaborate, 'my *head* . . .' but suddenly I felt very weary. I had evidently hit on a cow sacred even to the cynical Fox.

'Look,' he said, 'I'm not a *prude* or anything like that, but this . . .' he touched the ms with a cough which seemed to stifle a retch, '. . . I mean, *this* is the most . . . *grotesque* . . . *obscene* . . . well, I'd rather not even discuss it. Frankly, I think you're in very real need of psychiatric attention.'

'Do you think Hack will go for it?' I asked in perfect candour.

Fox averted his eyes and began to drum his fingers on the desk.

'Look, uh, I've got quite a bit of work to do this morning, so, you know, if you don't mind . . .'

'Gone too far, have I, Fox? Is that it? Maybe you're missing the point of the thing—ever consider that?'

'Listen,' said Fox stoutly, lips tightened, one finger raised in accusation, 'you show this . . . *this thing* to anybody else, you're liable to get a *big smack in the kisser*!' There was an unmistakable heat and resentment in his tone—a sort of controlled hysteria.

'How do you know I'm not from the CIA?' I asked quietly. 'How do *you* know this isn't a *test*?' I gave him a shrewd narrow look of appraisal. 'Isn't it just possible, Fox, that this quasi-indignation of yours is, in point of fact, simply an *act*? A *farce*? A *charade*? An *act*, in short, to *save your own skin*!?!'

He had succeeded in putting me on the defensive. But now, steeped in Chink poet cunning, I had decided that an offence was the best defence, and so plunged ahead. 'Isn't it true, Fox, that in this parable you see certain underlying homosexual tendencies which you unhappily recognise in yourself? Tendencies, I say, which to confront would bring you to the very brink of, uh, 'fear and trembling', so to speak.' I was counting on the Kierkegaard allusion to bring him to his senses.

'You crazy son of a bitch,' he said flatly, rising behind his desk, hands clenching and unclenching. He actually seemed to be moving towards me in some weird menacing way. It was then I changed my tack. 'Well listen,' I said, 'what would you say if I told you that it wasn't actually *me* who did that, but a Chinese poet? Probably a Commie . . . an insane Commie-fag-spade-Chinese drug fiend. Then we could view it objectively, right?'

Fox, now crazed with his own righteous adrenalin, and some-what encouraged by my lolling helplessly in the chair, played his indignation to the hilt.

'Okay, Buster,' he said, towering above me, 'keep talking, but make it good.'

'Well, uh, let's see now . . .' So I begin to tell him about my experience with the Red-Split. And speaking in a slow, deliberate, very serious way, I managed to cool him. And then I told him about an insight I had gained into Vietnam, Cassius Clay, Chessman, the Rosenbergs, and all sorts of interesting things. He couldn't believe it. But, of course, no one ever really does—do they?

THE LONG BOOK

Alexander Trocchi

For some years the most important novelist writing about drugs and drug usage in Britain was Alexander Trocchi (1925–1984) whose drug experiences and addiction to heroin form the basis of his superb novel, Cain's Book, *which has been the subject of both controversy and prosecution. Trocchi, who like Terry Southern was generous with comments and suggestions for this book, considered himself in many ways a disciple of William Burroughs and Allen Ginsberg and indeed appeared with them at artistic gatherings (reading poetry with Ginsberg) and on forums discussing drug morality. He lived and worked in Glasgow, where he was born; Paris, where he studied on a postgraduate scholarship; and London, where he finally settled. In* Cain's Book *he gives a memorable picture of his years of addiction in both Europe and America: 'To be a junkie is to live in a madhouse. Laws, police forces, armies, mobs of indignant citizenry crying mad dog. We are perhaps the weakest minority which ever existed; forced into poverty, filth, squalor, without even the protection of a legitimate ghetto. There was never a Wandering Jew who wandered farther than a junkie without hope. Always moving. Eventually one must go where the junk is and one is never certain where the junk is, never sure that where the junk is is not the anteroom of the penitentiary.' His experiences with drugs go far wider than heroin, however, and he has written of his use of marijuana: 'an ambiguous drug which can induce control or hysteria, and sometimes a terrifying and enervating succession of moods'—mescaline, and LSD: 'objects of perception become intrusive in an electric way'—and cocaine: 'the perceiving turns inwards'.*

Since his death in 1984, discussion of Trocchi's place in modern literature has provoked widely differing opinions. William Burroughs called him 'a critical and pivotal figure in the literary world of the 1950s and '60s', while one of the leading Scottish poets, Hugh McDiarmid, dismissed him as 'cosmopolitan scum—a writer of no literary consequence whatsoever'. Certainly, he is remembered in Britain as a highly controversial figure and has been described variously as 'junkie, pimp, outsider, Scottish beat, literary outlaw, visionary, philosopher, underground organiser and antique book dealer'. His other novel, Young Adam *(1957), an existential thriller about a rootless antihero which was inspired by Albert Camus's* The Outsider, *is due to be republished in his native Scotland.*

As a revolutionary thinker in the field of social causes as well as that of narcotics and stimulants, it is perhaps not surprising to find that Trocchi's story for this collection is a futuristic fantasy. In some ways it reminds one of William Burroughs' The Soft Machine *and* The Nova Express, *but these apart it is a visionary tale of some excellence.*

*   *   *

In my study of drugs (I don't pretend for a moment that my sole interest in drugs is to study their effects . . . To be familiar with this experience, to be able to attain, by whatever means, the serenity of a vantage point 'beyond' death, to have such a critical technique at one's disposal—let me say simply that on my ability to attain that vantage point my own sanity has from time to time depended)—in my study of drugs I have been forced to run grave risks, and I have been stymied constantly by the barbarous laws under which their usage is controlled. These crude laws and the social hysteria of which they are a symptom have from day to day placed me at the edge of the gallows leap. I demand that these laws be changed.

Cain's Book, 1961

In his fortieth year, according to the most exact sigmatic information, Joseph Necchi, alias the sexistential—one of the last men—inherited the earth. At least, it seemed to him he had done so, or was doing so, and would be doing so, momently, thereafter. He discovered the decision in himself there and then, wherever and whenever it was, and felt it and himself from then on renewed, at each bright moment of confirmation. 'It is here and now,' he wrote to another of his shadow kind in another land. 'It is happening. The future is our inheritance.'

The Long Book (shades will recognise the noumenal foetus of the sigmatic toilet roll) was constructed of and on behalf of what has come to be known as the 'invisible insurrection' — 'God-speed all cosmonauts of inner space!' cried Necchi in the falseteeth of some manufacturers of moral rearmaments, and would there and then have mounted the naked lady in the McEwan Hall, like the rampant ram he was, had not the lion in him been tempered by his foxy Roman ancestry. Old fox of Rome that he was! And inventor of numberless identities ... When asked by a critic, to whom was he referring when he spoke of 'they'?—he replied: 'When they come into my room and find me with my eyes closed, for them I am asleep: they are the enemies of contemplation, dull motor-ataxiane cut off from the Himalayan horizons of the third eye ...'

The idea was finally committed to writing in this period following the roman's return from the United States, the deed done in the living in that part of his permanent temporary quarters given over to the holy-of-holies, deftly done and tentatively, amongst substances, instruments, and engines of experiment. Aaram had gone into the futique-shop caper in sheer desperation, having tried during devious wanderings amongst natives of divers contemporaneous civilisations in sondrie laundes, high and low, far and wide, north and south, east and west, tried, even laboured under effort, to live his life freely, without absolute commitment to one and all of the patent relativities teeming about him. These he would have liked to stuff into the paper bag in which he kept his spike and his condom, a piece of agate, a small dung-coloured nob of the finest hashish, and two thighs in rut for his fleshwriting. But it rained and the bag burst, and another bag after that, and indeed he could never find the right container. Moreover, there was always some joe gander or plooknecked customs artificer to interrogate him along thirty feet of trestle tables through his flyman's telescope, and, alas! he had found himself pressured persistently in all places, in cities and in prisons and in villages and in hospitals, to define himself clearly in terms familiar to the rudest of those about him, and to act accordingly, on pain of death or harsh confinement. And there was ever the problem of the unorthodox container. If it didn't burst, it farted!

Inevitably, wherever he paused to acquaint himself with the local situation did he encounter men who had got themselves into groups to govern as did kings and parliaments according to tradition. This group and its appointed vicars, in whatever land, were the guardians of that land's conventions. And the scene around our Soris was, by all extant conventional standards, unusual, and while a Martian might have considered it less outlandish than, for example, the works and worship of the congregation of the first presbyterian tabernacle in Little Frankenstein, Arkansas and in terms of raw process altogether more logical (as ripe pregnancy after lust), vicars of all established denominations smelled the winds of change and tightened hempen guyropes.

General Apathy KBE would have no truck with Martians, whom he regarded as outsiders by definition (can we really tolerate green pricks in our white runts?) and the general was quoted by the society columnist of the botulist bugle of hysteria pogromshire as saying of Joseph Necchi, 'This man is a notorious sexistential, and unrepentant pervert, and a self-confessed dopefiend, one million of the d. . . breed which, secretly and with malice aforethought, has been landing during the past few decades on this unsuspecting planet . . .'

'Like blowflies on shit,' Coriolanus said to a visiting dean.

For more than two decades, indeed, the uncategorical imperative had been flaring like a (black) beacon across continents.

Now, Daedalus had noticed that every such group without exception assumed the power of life and death over individuals who chanced to be or go within its jurisdiction. Wherever he went, therefore, Eros did his utmost, within the limits of sigmatic expedience, to initiate the processes of operation outcry. Sometimes, and more frequently with the passing of the years, it was his good fortune gradually to discover such processes, begun before his arrival. Then he felt himself invaded by a kind of brainwave . . .

How many zealots could we have? At present we had nearly fifty thousand: sufficient for the day. It seemed the assets in this element of war were ours. If we realised our raw materials and were apt with them, then climate, railway, desert and technical weapons could also be attached to our interests. The Turks were stupid; the Germans behind them dogmatical. They would believe that rebellion was absolute like war, and deal with it on the analogy of war. Analogy in human things was fudge, anyhow: and war upon rebellion was messy and slow, like eating soup with a knife.

T. E. Lawrence

120 planes bomb N. Vietnam from Ratten Tot (Lushington, March 31). Today has seen the greatest air activity of the Quietcon War. While over 120 United Brutes and South Vietnamese planes were bombing six separate targets in the North, 70 other planes were dropping tons of napalm bombs and barrels of fuel oil in an attempt to burn out Tryiton guerrillas from a nest near New York . . .

Hon. Agatha Hardon's blue eyes moved gently on to her corn-flakes. No news, of course. Just the usual good morning scream implying a woman had far more to defend these days than the garters to whose protection Victoria Regina had dedicated her widowhood. Blonde Bunny will hitchhike to Mars. Male must be Martian. The ghost of the late empress lingered on, however, and many women of her granddaughters' generation still emulated her. Murder, panic, and corruption reported in the News of the Church. Permeability amongst the miles and miles of news-print. But, in fact, few minds were capable of absorbing and being affected by the flesh and blood behind the print. People were stunned by too much of it. Click! they turned off: in self-defence. (Turn on cooler!) It was true what the sexistential had said to her the previous night: that we were condemned by our

own institutions, about history's being 'amok'. Visit one's MP
for reassurance? He'll sell us a policy? So, most women returned
to defending their garters, as excitingly and as profitably as possible. And some committed suicide. Most of the men of her
acquaintance never seriously considered the problem. And if they
were carried to that point in a conversation, they remembered
that polite-conversation-is-never-serious or they lapsed into
the God-gave-us-courage-and-hope-routine, bishops' banalities.
And women performed polite bird-motions to sustain their men.
So that it seemed jack the raper would be top of the pops eternally.
At least it had seemed so until the evening her room-mate,
Ophelia D'Arce, forgot an appointment and Agatha twanged like
a supple English longbow at the touch of the sexistential's flat
front.

Hon. Agatha Hardon remembered that occasion most vividly
as she lifted the cornflakes off a yard away across the table and
poked her spoon into fresh grapefruit. Ophelia D'Arce was her
lifelong friend and some-time lover. 'A really super girl'.

'Miss Agatha Hardon,' said the sexistential sweetly to her there
in that long room.

'Then I too shall come to the point,' said she, darkly.

When their smouldering passions had inhabited one body and
were (warmly) subsided, she told him what Ophelia had said to
her an hour earlier as she collected herself and dashed out of the
flat:

'Of God, I forgot!' said Ophelia all of a sudden, raising her
slender hand from her soft sweet amazonian heats where the thick
slabs of her powerful thighs came together at the wild fulcrum
of her lower abdomen sticky and stenching after wenching on a
bed of burgundy grapes. Agatha's body remembered the other
body soft and haired as silken gooseberries against the netherlip.
'How could I forget! I was to be astride rat-Levy's blue mug
with no drawers on and dripping, my dear, at eight o'clock sharp!
It is after nine, in case my darling failed to notice, and here I
am wallowing like a pig in your damn grapebath and dyed redder
than any wife of MacBeth! £500 is at stake!'

'Cash?'

'Cash. You could have ordered white grapes, Ag, you luscious slut!'

'And forfeit the blood?'

'Bugger the bloody blood!'

'£500?'

'£500.'

'It's not enough,' Agatha said, turning on her belly amongst broken, bruised grapes. 'The man can't wait to get his moustache between your legs. You said so yourself. His lapels are stiffened with $100 bills, remember?'

'He's not a rat, my darling, because he likes to be prepared for pogroms, nor indeed because he likes to prise my marble pillars apart with that blue chin of his; he's a rat because he's furtive when he bucks. He always turns off all the lights before he begins. I never know which direction he'll come from. And then, there he is, just a shadowy hulk, quivering like a rat beside me. Rat-Levy, yr Ophelia D'Arce is on her way!' And the big pretty pink girl stepped under the shower.

'*I Am A Prostitute*, by the Hon. Agatha Hardon SVP,' said Agatha, selecting a large unbroken purple grape from her fruity bedding, and plopping it unbroken through lovely lips into her mouth. The bow of the lips, the set of the face, the painted eyes, were Egyptian.

With the steam rising from the shower came the immaculate voice of Ophelia D'Arce, singing the latest pop hit:

> 'I lie here wondering
> about it all, how
> it wasn't like that at all.
> How you bucked me thru
> the slit in my overall . . .'

And then: 'Do you know, Ag, what that louse Fink said about my apparent addiction to Jewish men? He said it was racial prejudice! My subconscious, I suppose, is a kind of Auschwitz . . .'

'How do you feel, darling, when you've sold yr body, or a short lease anyway?' said Agatha at the bundling steam.

Huskily, 'Rather depends on what one's had for dinner, doesn't it?' Ophelia replied.

'I miss Phee,' Agatha said now across the breakfast table to Ferdinand.

'Men turn away from the implications of their thoughts like commercial travellers from their bastards,' he replied. 'Phee? Ophelia D'Arce? Yes. Why don't you invite her to come to Tangiers?'

'Do you think she would come?'

'She might. And, not to shirk the implication of my own thoughts on the subject: I can't imagine anything nicer than to be the filling of a sandwich with Phee and yrself as the bread.'

'Sam Sandwich spread, soon him dead,' said Agatha demurely. 'Him dead, him washed.'

'Such waste as can has already taken place,' retorted the sexistenial. 'Let us send at once for Ophelia D'Arce!'

'God,' said Godfrey, 'is always in the first person, like a man at crap.' He had been telling Agatha about a book he was writing; the act he was perpetrating: *The Long Book* (or *The Addict in the White House*). 'It is of the future of continents conceived in the urinals of my pure heart,' he had said. They were lying on the low round bed, twelve feet in diameter, which stood at the end of the studio. They had gone there after a swim after breakfast. Beside them, set into the nearest wall, was the red plastic face of the radio, nine inches high, three feet long. 'Sick, sack, suck a bum's abuck!' said the announcer. 'Superior thin vaseline: Axel's Axlegrease: makes buggering easy as peasebrose?'

'What station's that?' Agatha said.

'Mars,' he replied. It occurred to Hamlet as he lay beside Agatha, that thinking, silent or out loud, was ineffectual, the way writing was. Baked, fried, or steelblue and gleaming from the hook, the mackerel was dead however it was presented, nor even was 'mackerel' outside 'my' thinking. *I* am in more senses than one an 'idealer'. I am a kind of funeral director of what is essentially wordless. Each thought is a coffin for what previously lived. Black coffins, white coffins, coffins with brass handles . . . what's the difference? I bury things even when I praise them. Jean-Paul

Sartre out of Mark Anthony. How did I ever think I could get nearer to things if I thought out loud, nearer, that is, than if I were to write my thoughts down? No matter how spontaneous my utterance, each word is a nail in the coffin of the corpse I wished to touch undead, unsymbolised. I deal in ideal or not at all. Nevertheless, I often thought ... no, I often felt ... If I thought out loud and spontaneously I'd get nearer to something, by a process of overspill, evade the censor, catching myself out. Catching whom out? The same sordid half-existence who sat down early this morning and took a fix? *Que suis-je?* A pseudentity out of inertia with a thirst to be. A microscopic speck of consciousness on the dark tide of unbeing, with athlete's foot? A swift fix makes nonsense of whatever definition, rings an epistemological bell. Still, that is the kind of question that interests me, the illegitimate question, the 'meaningless' one, the one in which is involved a host of ambiguities, a morass of symbols, a swarm of bees, word chasing sense, sense chasing words, and out of which, suddenly, as a ship out of fog ... an image, a crisis, a sound ...

On. Again. Along a road, there is still a road, the same road, blank and categorical like a state highway in the desert, and friends as old as lizards with their stone grimaces ... how swiftly they scuttle when surprised! That isn't what I meant to say, not at the beginning when I sat myself down. It's the same road, different, bars of particulars, unfolding itself towards the red suppuration of sin at the long blue horizon, which might be volcanic, or a burning man. At the road's edge, a few scrub oaks, stones of many colours, quartz, feldspar, fluorite, garnet, gold. In the desert emotions take on a nakedness that could be offensive in the salon. There was, as I remember, dust clinging to the woman's thighs which had been wet and weren't any longer, and it clung there as wet sand clings, forming ridges against her white flesh, a glinting leafedge against the soft northern city-protected loins of a city woman who kept on her nylons and her garterbelt for ye oulde prospector who sprinkled her fine melon-belly with the gold-dust of his strike ... Goldenballs Gannon of I-o-way, dogone died a year later in Las Vegas, Nev., in the stroke of his passion . . . Jesus Christ! the oulde fart's croaked! At the beginning, her first thought for insects that crawled . . . before she was persuaded, because she remembered the day just off the highway between Nogales and Guaymas, and the exhilaration at having escaped at last across the border into what might have been another century, and the climb down over the embankment at the side of the road to the small bridge under which we lay with our naked legs entwined, when suddenly she felt the red ants and saw them move like a minute river of blood over her skin. There is nothing that is not in some way or other ambiguous, dialectical, in time. It was along the road these moments at which I was out of time, at which the world was like a perfection at my senses, whether it was a woman or a stone, it was those moments which provided me with a hieroglyphic out of which I was able to construct it again; and it is so even now again as I go on.

Igor chose the desert to begin with, not because anything began or came to an end there, but because of its relative emptiness, because, especially in remembering, he didn't wish to be at once overcome with a profusion of things, much as he supposed Descartes had chosen his *cognito*: to have an apodeictic posture from which to be going on. He said: 'There's a specific character in all the acts in the life of a man, an awful sameness in all his various situations. Even his accidents are affinitive. And every man is alone in a night world in which the beacons of responsibility have gone out.'

'In Las Vegas,' Ophelia had said, 'there's nothing like gold for correct friction.'

This is the long book. I should say: this will be (or, this is becoming) the long book. For what form this book will take enters my conscious mind gradually as it is written. I have the feel of it, and, in that sense, could be said to know what it is about, but whether it will lie, a bible in a brothel, a textbook in a factory for human engineering, or hang, a toilet roll in the lavatories of the enlightened . . . certain historical facts and factories seem to be beyond my immediate control, Dr Kildare . . . where was Noah without the flood?

'When can you let us have your next novel?' Jeremiah's publisher had asked him.

'Call it a spade, not a shovel,' Kubla Khan replied. 'If you'd really dug where I was at in the last, you wouldn't keep asking that question.'

'I do wish you would be serious, Bla. I'm running a business.'

'It's called *Notes Towards the Tactical Revaluation of the Human Process*,' Necchi replied. 'And it should be printed on toilet rolls and hung like an air-freshener in the lavatories of all lands.'

'Poof!' said Pottle the publisher. 'That's old hat! Didn't someone do something like that before somewhere . . . I'm sure I heard . . . now . . . who was it . . . ? I . . . ?

'Sir Izal Germicide,' Necchi said, 'and *imperm'eable*, as I remember.'

'Lionel, it wouldn't sell!' Pottle insisted, 'and anyway, the bookshops wouldn't stock it. You know how they treated *Cain's Book* . . .'

'Pottle, it is precisely because they have damned and insulted and labelled as obscene and caused to be burned by the public executioner the fealthy dorty wordes of yr humble's . . . I demand the privacy of a lavatory where I can tickle yr balls for you when you're alone with yr wig off and yr bum down, if you take my meaning?'

'Mmmm,' Pottle pondered, placing one small pink crocus-like hand at his round chin and smiling in his blue eyes, remembering the naked lady he had caused to be transported in flagrant sin and trembling, history of literary supplement. Again he saw the outraged headlines. 'Who would print it, Mathieu? I doubt if it could be done . . .'

'Thy will be done, Pottle,' Mark said. 'Don't you see the relevance, how fitting the toilet roll? Nasty man banished to lavatory. Shine a bright light in the crazy corridors of those toilet-trained consciences? Just a wee bit? Like a new hymn:

> Jock lost his sporran
> is dangling free
> God cares for he . . .

A toilet roll now would be a best seller, Puttis. Evil Epigrams
Encapsulated, Publishers. Build a fire under the turkey-necked
bastards!'

'It's all very well for you,' Pottle now protested. 'You can
simply take off for Tangiers if things get out of hand. I can't.
I'd look very silly pushing a barrowload of toilet rolls!'

For the sexistential the long book was an act, a making, an
outbreak, a measured scream. He might have said: this book is
written to kill, or, less melodramatically: I keep a log. He might
have called it *The Case of the Proscribed Informations*, the long
book, this further gambit in the boardless chase-game wherein it
was his misfortune to discover himself already at play and with
no knowledge of the relevant dimensions. But Pottle had required
a title at once, and Joe, after all, had Ag to think of. She required
her scents and her greasepaints. And her golden nipple-cups he
found charming, as well as her delicately wrought bellybutton-
stud. The long book it was therefore, or would be.

'Now it is a game I am going to play,' Necchi might have
quoted, if he had known the rules ... but I should have been
lying, perhaps smiling one of my finer false faces. Was it in
fact or fiction that I creased her massive centrale, moving my
carcassone down through her pziroknees into her softs' pain?
The distinction has grown confused over a quarter of a century.
The problem of truth and falsity I bequeath to those who come
after me along with my second sharpest hypodermic needle.
Meanwhile, I should like a man to be alone when he reads this
document: he should imagine an oval of glazed, cream-coloured
enamel chipped black at one edge by unknown vandals, its surface
anastomosed by cracks and written on in the usual urinal brown,
a little plaque screwed to the door in front of him where he sits
in the cubicle of a public toilet where he has no one to turn to
nor caper for. Then he will not use me as a foil, at least until he
has read what I have written (the which he could be grateful for,
having no other reading matter), or what he thinks I have written,
or what he thinks he thinks I have written, or ... but in my
universe where no road leads to Rome, where every avenue
becomes a road becomes a path becomes a track and eventually

undisturbed sand, such regressions once implied may be taken
for granted, although nothing else can.

(When they appeared it was as Romana in the streets.) The man
then, should be alone; each member of a jury can avoid my gaze
and, at the subsequent conclave, evade the real encounter and
insolently condemn me. As for my judge, let him come down
from where he picks his nose behind his magisterial bench and
expose his short hairs. All that symbolic paraphernalia of conventional power, lumber out of the past, is anachronism, stage scenery for old arguments. The cripple can't walk until he dispenses
with his crutches. The man at crap is at my level, squatting more
or less comfortably on his naked haunches, at serious purpose
with himself and beyond equivocation in his need to rid himself
of the accumulated poisons of the living process.

> The slack white body
> of yr dead Aunt Peg
> had a pink confection
> for a face, the day
> they buried her.
> —Gone in her prime,
> like yr gin and lime!
> Candy kisses . . .
> Meet a dark stranger!

As for those dicte of koanst any immodesty is in the reverber-
ations of the mind which contemplates them. What kind of hocus-
pocus ever led men to think otherwise? Ponder these things before
you speak of improper suggestions and complain to the attendant
of a flagrant obscenity in Cubicle Zed.

'When you speak of the "cannabis problem",' Peter went on,
placing the wee green-black turd of some of the finest hashish
of Asia Minor on the delicate curve of Ag's creamsweet abdomen,
'I take it you mean that of assuring the supply of fine-quality
goods, of improving the yield and quality of the hemp plant in
both hemispheres, of evolving efficient grading methods, and so

on? Did I tell you that this piece came all the way from the secret cellar of Genghis Khan?' And his forehead fell forward and down until it pressed against the nut of hashish and the lozenge of his lips closed like a cockle to the cream.

'Eat me!' said the Hon. Ag with a laughing husky groan, and she raised one sleek thigh like the neck of a white mare in the gold of the late morning sunlight. Her hand stroked his tangled hair.

From a narrow slit in the masonry at the other side of the court the lens of a powerful telescope protruded. In the high heat of the midday sun Finck, German agent of the yellow peril (alias Dr Yu No Fok), was still at work. His employer was not interested in the prevailing meteorological conditions in northwest Africa. If the sexistential had been at the north pole, Finck would have been expected to be there, 'tapping' him . . . Follow that iceberg!

For it had long been suspected by the repressive elements of various governments in the world that the man who was known as the sexistential was engaged in activities which amounted to sedition on a global scale, but most deviously and with great subtlety, since up till now, and in spite of the energies of divers public prosecutors, he had been seen to commit no actual felony, not once in all his travels which, in themselves, were highly suspicious in the opinion of upright men; for they served no obvious purpose. Had Finck not already produced as evidence a certain scrap of paper retrieved from Necchi's wastepaper basket on which the following had been noted?—'New York, 1960. The hero as junkie, confounder of conformities, sinker of moral ducks, alone with his twilight detergent, in his original posture, in his every shuddering act, he resists his times. With the bad fiction of international politics he wipes his pile-encrusted arse. Can't buy vaseline these days without a prescription. (Was that true?) Where would the Empire City be without its pariahs, the blue geek with his sliding walk, slobbering the poetry of his liver-loose lips at the sanitation squad sent to dispose of him?

'Where he lay on a stoop, a hoarfrost of his peculiar perspiration, snailglint, and five cigarette stubs left over from a previous work of fiction lying extinguished in their own long ash. It got dark a short while ago a long while ago and the fog and the night wrapped themselves up in each other until suddenly under the pale yellow cone of light from the lamp-post, transparent parvenu amongst my sensations, is myself.'

The man (and here Finck placed a question-mark in parentheses) was elated all the time. It was unnatural. You would call him a failure . . . a man who idled away his time, more often than not under the influence of some drug or other, many of them obtained, Finck was ready to swear, from some underworld acquaintance, a certain West Indian most probably, yes, the man sat or sprawled all day, fiddling with a tape-recorder and composing articles which were often obscene and perhaps subversive. How, with his life based on such foul delights, did the fellow contrive to appear elated all the time? The man, too, showed no regard whatsoever for money, was up to his neck in debt, and unemployed so long as to be unemployable. And yet this Uranus seemed to prosper . . . something was wrong somewhere, that was to say, not right . . . and Finck hinted at some dark purpose as yet unrevealed. It was his (Finck's) business to penetrate that purpose and to expose it in such a way that the more liberal elements would be forced to side in this matter with the ultra-conservatives, whose secret agent the yellow peril was. And so the telescope tilted downwards now to take in the yard into which an Arab was now leading a camel. '*Gott in Himmel!*' breathed the intrepid agent as the telescope came to focus on the face of the man who walked there below in the yard. 'It is Dahou himself!' Finck dashed down the stone stairs three at a time to the cellar where his secret radio transmitter was cunningly installed.

'It is over ten years now since Midhou left me in Athens,' Sir Victor said to the Hon. Ag. The lovely lady was in the process of affixing the ruby stud to the whorl of flesh at her navel.

'Must you dress, darling?' said the sexistential when he noticed. He noticed too that her posture was most alluring and simul-taneously felt his centre of gravity shift downwards like an invisible sea towards his crotch. The smoky blue runt was a strange flower in the white grotto of her groin.

Joseph Necchi had begun to experiment with visual objects in a serious way in the middle-Fifties, first in Paris and then later when he was living in California near the Mojave Desert. Of course, he had always been concerned with visual experience, though, until now, his reputation had rested mainly on the excellence of his prose. And even during his editorship of *Mainliner* (the Anglo-American literary quarterly published in Paris in the early Fifties), he was already constructing his habitat about him.

He had owned a tiny cubelike room in Montparnasse, two minutes away from the Dome where latterly he had come to make most of his mysterious 'connections': a studio, monk's cell and buckpad, where at any hour he might quiet the ferocious wild beast in his loins, a holy place in short, the bed-centrepiece of which was an altar. 'I'm a real holy bucker already,' he said once in the Bronx. His bookcases were a multicoloured structure of variable planes built to allow him to read efficiently when horizontal (a frequent posture for an inveterate smoker of hashish and opium). An important prop this, it resembled in some respects the portable pulpit with which Necchi sometimes confounded the Enemy on the night streets of Manhattan. Mounted on it, with paints, brushes, and various masterly 'futiques' in front of him, he considered himself, and usually was, improbable enough to offset and outflank all the facts of New York City. Of course it could only be a temporary measure, and in the end he had fled out of that land, wisely, and in the nick of time. The facts, he knew, were breathing down his neck.

He had returned via Montreal, the Newfoundland icebanks, round the northern tip of Scotland one early translucent dawn, to the ancient granite city of Aberdeen, and thence by way of Glasgow (city of his 'birth') to London, a thin grey figure, lamppost or ghost, the idea of the *coup-de-monde* close under eyelids, an electronic load, an unwritten book, a plan in four dimensions, a shadow one, taking as given that complex of informations called London 196– as raw material for his engraver's tool, and calling at last, finally, for poet's rule.

'Weenie, weedy, weakie,' said William the Conqueror as he stepped ashore at Aberdeen. He had half-expected an escort on arrival . . . a small black car perhaps (in contrast to the gleaming white spaceships of Las Vegas), with two tall fellows in plain clothes.

'Niatzschie?' one of them would say.

Discovered!

'Nothing concealed abt yr parson? In a hollow tooth? Behind yr foreskin? Up the old bungho?'

Smelling the seat of a bully's body, the sexistential decided to turn off, and, availing himself of the martian technique of elision, he demateralised and regrouped his faculties alone in a context with no men and only his own deceit to confront, in his own bottle, airy or earthy, as it happened.

The book Xerxes was flipping through was in French . . . a book which around 1948 had made a lasting impression upon him. Translating as he went: 'You're a coward,' I said. 'you're a motherbucker. The fuzz is still too good to you. One of these days you'll really be licking their boots. Maybe they'll go visit you where you're bagged and shove their pricks up yr arse.' Said to Stiletana or Michaelis? Anyway, 'an old and evil presence from an old and evil cave,' as his friend, the dean, put it. And that led, naturally, to his thinking abt the dean. And he remembered saying to him: 'Cut up or boil down, it doesn't seem to matter what technique so long as it doesn't become an institution.' The dean agreed with him. Wherever he went Yehudi found individuals whose posture was, at times anyway, metacategorical as his own. There was the ground of his tentative optimism. He was not the only man who knew he was alone.

The barbecue was executed at noon precisely on that day in a secret chamber somewhere in the bowels of the Institute. It was supervised by Dr Hare Q. Kildare, prominent medical telecaster who headed the disciplinary board at the Institute and who, at a recent general meeting of the AMA was highly commended for a speech entitled: 'The Health of the Citizen under Free Enterprise', in which he stressed the importance in a democratic society of a man's paying his own medical bills, issued a warning against foreign bodies of all kinds, at the same time calling for a strict international ban on narcotics as a *must* for civilisation as we know it. In their various official and unofficial capacities, the following lords, ladies, and gentlemen were present: the Reverend Filing Delinquent of Lisreggub, Prof. Horat Nesel, Obersturm-führer Doktor Mengele of Auschwitz Sanatorium, Lord Jeremy Stoppit, Mrs Remember Gomorrah, and the elegant Countess Dracula, sophisticated spouse of the Enemanian Ambassador, which lady herself is recognised as a noted student of moral science, and who studied under the late Commissioner Manslayer.

The jolt or brainbouncer was what is considered average in this kind of case, Rev. Filing Delinquent informed his colleagues, slightly more than is ordinarily employed in current European practice, considerably less than that recommended in Ambassador Dracula's country.

'Enough,' concluded our distinguished cleric, 'to dissolve neutral tissue without causing body-odour.'

At the third jolt the patient's body was seen to shudder like a tall jelly within the leather harness, and a wisp of blue smoke issued from red nostrils, a reaction generally regarded as a symptom of what, in technical nomenclature, is called 'reintegration'. The patient reintegrated slowly, the shuddering subsided gradually over a period of two and a half hours, after which he was returned to the deep freeze as a precaution against pong.

It was the practice, Dr Kildare pointed out to those present, to wait three days before attempting to estimate the results of the operation, since further changes not unlike those of terrestrial subsidence (earthquakes, volcanic eruptions, etc.) were often met with during a period of up to forty-eight hours after the barbecue. The patient's eyeballs, which had been driven out of their sockets by the electric brainbouncer, had a vaguely cooked look which, explained the eminent telecaster, could have sinister implications, and this naturally made him reluctant to predict success or failure at the present time.

Mrs Remember Gomorrah spoke afterwards, calling for the stimulation of public interest in the various modes of electrocution. 'This poor fellow,' she declared, referring to the electro-cuted catatonic, 'is now no longer a menace to himself or to others.' She concluded her remarks by insisting upon the urgent need for the immediate segregation of that portion of the popu-lation which was infected. In this she was eagerly seconded by Obersturmführer Doktor Mengele who offered to place his sana-torium at the disposal of the committee. His engineers, he averred, were already studying the possibility of chain treatment.

Dr Hare (Bunny to his friends) Q. Kildare returned to his study with the other members of the committee, and when they were all provided with some fine dry sherry which he kept for such occasions, he began: 'Trouble was, though I'm reluctant to say it, the man failed to distinguish between two kinds of perspiration, the physical kind and the mental kind. Science shows that in the glands of the mature male and the glands of the mature female perspiration caused by anxiety emits an offensive odour. For two thousand years man has sought to avert this embarrassment. Poor Cleopatra had to spend twelve hours a day in milk baths and having expensive oils and elixirs rubbed into her skin, particularly during political crises, and all to avoid what nowadays we call ... I am sure the ladies present will excuse me! ... bee-oh! Yes, body odour; like the poor, it has always been with us ... ha! Nevertheless (the forefinger of Kildare's right hand pointed trium-phantly up), with our modern techniques, in this instance, electric-shock therapy, we have devised a way to abolish all thought, and thus, Ladies and Gentlemen, all anxiety and the resultant offen-sive odours ...'

Polite exclamations, applause and a smattering of handclap-ping, interrupted all of a sudden by the ringing telephone.

Reluctantly, our eminent physician surrendered his captive audience and, with a gesture of impatience, lifted the pastel-pink receiver.

'Yu No Fok here!' a voice came urgently from the other end of the line. 'For Kildare the yellow peril immediately here speaks now, please!'

'This *is* Kildare, Dr Fok. Is there some trouble, sir?' he cupped his hand over the receiver and flashed a glance at his guests.

'Fok,' he said quietly to be the unvoiced question on their various faces, 'Central Security . . .'

His guests turned away discreetly to converse amongst themselves. Mengele addressed the Rev. Filing Delinquent: 'As I was saying earlier, Delinquent, fortunately I was able to expose that fool who accused me in short order. "Lies," I said. "All lies! You say we National Socialists made soap from murdered Jews. That is a patent falsehood. Fat is required to make soap and concentration camp victims were too thin for that!" Ha! You should have seen his face! I thought the lying swine was going to have a coronary!'

'Ha!' said the pigs, and 'Ho,' and 'Ha, ha! Hee, hee, hee! . . .'

'Trouble?' said the voice on the telephone, 'Yourself be judge, my friend. I haf reported to me by one of my best agents of a certain Mohammed Dahou. Thees man is arriving an hour ago in Tangiers . . . on one camel!'

'Good God!' Kildare exclaimed, and then, recovering his composure under the startled glances of his guests, he said in a firm voice: 'If this information is correct, we must inform General Apathy!'

The reunion of Mohammed Dahou and Zorro (alias Joseph Necchi alias the sexistential) took place towards the beginning of the end of the beginning (so to speak) in the Tangiers residence of the Honourable Agatha Hardon, runaway heiress, step-daughter of Mrs Remember Gormorrah, and niece of General Paralysis, esteemed colleague of Apathy KBE, of whom, each and every one of them, we shall hear more anon.

LET THE MICE IN

Brion Gysin

William Burroughs' story 'I Am Dying, Meester?', which appears
in the first part of this book, is an example of the 'cut-up' technique which he developed thanks to the pioneering work of Brion
Gysin (1922–   ), an expatriate American who has spent much
of his life travelling. Born in California, Gysin is a poet and
painter, perhaps most widely known through his friendship with
Burroughs and for his extraordinary novel The Process, published
in 1969, an extravaganza of magic, drugs and exotic experiences
set in the Sahara region. The narrator of the story, a devotee of
kif smoking, comments on one occasion, 'Eternity flows all about
me as I pull at my pipe, utterly silent under the stars.' Gysin first
met Burroughs in the United States before departing for Europe
and North Africa where, in Tangier, their paths crossed again.
For eight years Gysin explored the desert regions, painted the
wilderness scenery and also ran a restaurant in the Moroccan
city called 'The Thousand and One Nights', until bankruptcy
forced him to move to Paris. Here he encountered his old friend
again. 'Ran into grey-green Burroughs in the Place St Michel,'
he wrote later. ' "Wanna score?" he said. For the first time in
all the years I had known him, I really scored with him.'

    It was in the summer of 1959, while he was living at the famous
Beat Hotel, that Gysin chanced upon the idea of 'cut-ups' —
scissoring newspaper articles into sections and rearranging these
sections at random. Using this method he created his first work,
'Minutes To Go', which emerged with quite coherent and meaningful prose. Initially he saw nothing in the idea other than 'a
new method of writing that would allow literature to catch up

with painting by the use of collage'; Burroughs, however, when shown the result, sensed something much more important and started to put the idea to work on The Naked Lunch *which he had written in 1957. 'The main intention of Brion Burroughs and William Gysin has been to free the text from the page,' he explained later, 'to free the word from the surrounding matrix.' The following year the two men collaborated on a pair of short films,* Towers Open Fire *and* Cut-ups, *and for a time worked on a scenario for* The Naked Lunch.

Brion Gysin's ground-breaking work, 'Minutes to Go', was published in a pamphlet in 1959 and also broadcast on BBC Radio, bringing the 'cut-up' technique to a wider audience. A number of his other experimental pieces appeared in The Award Avant-Garde Gazette *and* Evergreen Review *before the publication of* The Process *which has become a cult book on both sides of the Atlantic. 'Let the Mice In' was written for* Evergreen Review *in 1969 and brilliantly evokes memories of his* kif-*fuelled maze of adventures in North Africa.*

*   *   *

Of *course* there was mushroom-magic, I assured him . . . right all the way across the North American steppe. He asked me to write him a paper on it and I did, for only *his* eyes: *Sight Without Glasses* . . . he practised it but that meant he had to put my paper right up to his nose, poor man . . . but he did have *another* kind of sight, like my grandmother had. Later, he asked my permission to send on my report to another old friend of his: Dr Forbach of Basel, the biggest chemical man in the game. LSD, you know, DMT, STP, BRB, that's my *Borbor* in a very unsophisticated form. I've been all the way up to BRB 144, I think . . . or *more*! Permutations of the formula I first worked on with Dr Forbach in Basel during my postgraduate year. That was all thanks to Huxley, I guess . . . and thanks to him, too, I suppose that I got a fat letter one day just before graduation, air mail from Basel, Switzerland, a rather business-looking envelope printed with the name of a famous pharmaceutical firm. There was no letter inside but a flat packet of very tiny pink pills marked PSYLOCIBIN. I picked up a paper on *psylocibin* in the lab . . .' *extract of mushrooms*'. It had been a long time. I could hardly wait to try them to see if *theirs* were as good as my old granny's and mine.

The Process, 1969

I talk a new language. You will understand.

I talk about the springes and traps of inspiration.

IN SPIRATION—what you breathe in. You breathe in words. Words breathe you IN. I demonstrate Thee, the Out-Word in action both visual and aural, racing away in one direction to sounds more concrete than music and, in the other, to paintings like television screens in your own head. I am better than Transducer for I show you own Interior Space.

In the beginning was the Word—been in You for a toolong time. I rub out the word. You in the Word and the Word in You is a word-lock like the combination of a vault or a valise. If you love your vaults, listen no further. I spin the lock on your Interior Space Kit. Prisoner: Come Out!

I sum on the Little Folk: music from the Mococcan hills proves the great god Pan *not* dead. I cast spells: all spells are sentences spelling out the word-lock that is You. Stop. Change. Start again. Lighten your own life sentence. Go back to childhood. Throw light on your little elves as they are in my magic picture 6 × 6 feet.

There will be projections in all dimensions while the recorded voice of Wm. Burroughs reads an incantation spelled out by him.

You will understand. I talk new springes and traps of inspiration. IN SPIRATION, what you breathe in. You breathe in words. Words breathe you IN. I demonstrate Thee, the Out-Word in words that breathe you in. Aural, racing away in one direction to action both visual and music and, in the other, to painting sounds more concrete screens in your own heads. I am better than like the televisions—your own Interior Space. Transducer for Eye show.

Was the word, Been in you for a too long. In the beginning, Word. You in the word and the word in You-Time. I rub out the combination on a vault or valise. '*If*' is a word-lock, like listen no further. I spin the lock on you love your vaults. It; Prisoner: come Out!

It's *your* Interior Space, folks—music from the Moroccan hills. I summon little Pan: *not* dead. I cast spells. All proves the great god spelling out the word-lock that is You. Spells are sentences again. Lighten your own life sentence. Stop. Change. Start. Throw light on your little elves as they go back to childhood. Are 6 × 6 feet. Are in my magic picturjections in all dimensions while the record there will be proproofs read in incantation; spelled out by the edited voice of Wm. Burro him.

Painting a picture re time and 6 × 6 during the act of an invocation for patient Moroccan to bow Chinese precede hills! Muto hirion. (sic) From the disappearance Gysin is *not* dead. Pan. Hurry. By the great god, Brion Gysin the torso of 1960. The mice in Gregory C.

A talk about the gees of stress and traps. An hour's length on sprint demonstrations of snouts and recorded visual sum of both, with projections and audible word. A pell of words. Magic space instead of sound pictures, shear peace. (Rub out the word and give more space.)

I will make a bow to the picture between your ears. The audience, too, appear into the picture. Visual words dye spells to shorten painting sentence. Fainting accompanied by our Act; by a spell from/of Wm. Burroughs . . . hm, spell cast by the voice of Wm. Burroughs' pa during painting a picture 6 × 6, the act or feat. Me to high Moroccan music from the disappear in hills. Is *not* dead. Hurry. Panrion Gysin.

By the great Go, Brion Gysin let Corso 1960 the mice in. Gregory Corso, 1960 aten Gysin the mice in Gregory. Spell cast by the ancient voice of Wm. Burroughs. Picture between your ears. Sound pictures and the word made bow to the audience.

How to paint out the visual and the audible give more space instead of spells for they shorten the picture. You will understand at hour's length.

I talk a new langhand, Gregory. Gysin let the mice in. 1960. I talk about the spiration gauge. You will understand Inspiration—who breathes in words. Springes and traps of words breathe in you—breathe you In. He Out-Word in hat you breathe in. Your action both visual and one direction. I demonstrate Thee. Racing away In, like the television to sounds more concrete other, to paintings aural. I am better than music in the Transducer for I show screams in your own head.

In the beginning, You for a tool on your own Interior Space Time. I rub out Thee and the Word in you *was* the Word—'been in' is a word-lock like Tilt or valise. If word. You in the Word, you love your vaults. Spin the lock on the combination on a vault—your Interior Space K! Listen no further.

I summon the little Moroccan hills. Prisoner: come Out. It proves the great god spells all the folk. Music from the spell-sentence that is You. Pan *not* dead. I can stop. Change. Start own life sentence. Spelling out the words, I go back to childhood. Little elves as they again. Lighten your O, you are in my magic picture. Throw light on your hell. There will be pro-ons while the records are 6 × 6 feet. Edited voice of Wm. Burroon spelled out by jections in all dimensions. Ughs reads an incantation. Invoke ancient Chinese precedent to bow three times and disappear into my picture.

During the act of painting picture, re time to bow Chinese, pre-invoked for a Moroccan potter (sic) said disappear in the picture.

Muto from the hirion hurry. Hill god Gysi and Gregorious Caius both of 960. Length in the torso abounded in the home sprint. Talk of it with Gees and traps forever audible word. Projected demonstration of snouts and wreck-pictures gives visual. Magic spell instead of sand gives bow to the end of words.

Stricture between your ears. I will shorten the painting sentence. The picture. How to paint and 'e'. The word is more shit. Me too had the mice in the hills who are *not* dead but dance. Invocation for paint in these preceding hills. Gysin is *not* dead. I will make an audience, too, snap at shortened painting sentence before I disappear into the hills. Fainting accompanied visual words, you will understand. A picture between the hills bowed to the Chinese audience—made an aural bow. They shorten the picture cast by an ancient voice between your ears. Demonstrations of little folks mice magic. Demonstration of corporeal projection during the disappearance. An ace instead of talk. Mirror magic and the writing that is you.

I talk a new laugh 1960. I talk about the Inspiration who breathes words in you. Your actions straight thee, racing away to concrete other, to pain in the Transducer for Eye. In the beginning, You Time. I rub out The. An 'In' is a word-lock like Word. You love your calf in a vault—your Interself.

I summon the little proofs of the great god sentence that is you. Started own life sentence in early childhood: Little elves in my magic picture.

I summon the Listener; come Out. It proves the great god speaks from spell-sentence that is you. Stop. Change. Start own life sentence. I go back to childhood. Little eleven year old, O, you are in my picture, O, you are as they again. Light in my magic picture. There will be harrowing light on your hell while the recorded voice of Wm. are at your feet. Like a cool towel of airforce over wrists and ankles. Burroons spelled out by Ons. Ughs read objections in all directions of sole incantation. I invoke to bow three ancient Chinese procedures to disappear into my picture.

The mice in, I will understand the traps of words in hat you wave in my direction. I, demon onto sounds more err than music, own your head. My own Interior Space a He word—been read. You in the combination further. Near. Come out. It sick from spells. Stop. Change. I go back to brighten you O you are. There will be blighted voice of Wm. on and on. Ughs reads Dent to bow three times and Gregory.

Gysin the Inspiration gauge. He is you in words. You, he's in words. Springes breathe you in. He Out—both visual and one dimensional; You In, like aural televisitings. I am betting I can show screams in your Owe-You for a tool. You're damned right; the word in you *was* 't' for Tilt or valise. If volts spin the lock on an interior space for K! Listen, O Moroccan hills.

Listen, O Moroccan hills! Poor prisohells, all the folk. Mustapha Pan *not* dead. I can spell out the words as they again. Light throw light on your hell.

I talk a new laugh at the mice In. I and Gregory. Gysin the 1960. I talk about the will understand spiration gauges. You, Inspiration—who bleats and traps of he's in words.

Springes words breathe in you—the word in that you breathe in you. He Out breathe In.

He Out breathe In your auto-rection. I demonstrate both visual and one dimension state thee. Racing away on sounds more Yin, like the televisions concrete other, more painful than music and things aural. I am better in the Transducer for I own head.

In the beginning, Your own Interior Spaced the Word in you. It *was* T Time. I rub out Thee and He Word. Spin the lock on Word, you love your veal, the combination on a vault, your Interior further.

I summon the littler; come out. It proves the great god spick from the spells. Pan *not* dead. I can speel the sentence that is you. You will understand. In the beginning—You time, I rub out a word-lock, like love your vaults. From the Moroccan can cast spells. All lock that is You. Demonstrate breath you in life sentence. I talk new springs of what you breathe the You in. Both aural and visual are concrete screens in you-he television—your own show.

Been in you for a toolong the word, and the word in a vault or valise. If I, I spin the lock on you . . . Out!

Superior Space Folk. Music, little Pan, *not* dead. God spelling out the words again—speeling out the hills. Light your own. Throw light on your 6 × 6 feet.

I summon the god-lit sentence, that life sentence that is early, is you. Started own childhood. Little structure of elves in magic pie. Ten, come out. It proves I summon the lilies, the great god sentence that is you. Speaks from the spell. I go back to childhood to start life sentencehood. Little eleven, my picture, O you are as year old! O, you are in they again! Light!

There will be harrowing in my magic picture. Light of hell and the voice of Wm. are at your wrists and ankles through all the recorded feet. Like a cool over wrists and ankles. Towels of airforce hold you back. I, in Chinese calm, proceed to painting.

Pictures to disappear in will understand the traps. Eye demon on to see you wave in my direction sounds more Her than He word. My own Interior Space music own your head. You in the corner, come out. It change. I go back sick from spells. Stop brightening your O—be blighted voice of Wm. You are. You, he's breathe you in. He Out in words. Springes both visual and one dimensional. You things. I am betting on your Owe-You for a Two. I can scream along. You're heard. I can hear you. Tit for tat, damned right. If volts spin locks on Interior Space, listen, O Mococcan hills!

Listen, O Moroccans; all the folk! In the hills poor prisoner Mustapha Pan is not dead. Words as he died. I can Spell them out again. Poor prisoned, I can spell out your hell. And the mice in it. I and thee will understand sporadic bleats and taps of his in you—the word in thee. Your own interior spaced out the He and Thee words. The combination on a word, you love your vested interior further. Come out; you can. It proven Pan *not* dead. You will understand. I word-lock, like love-you spells. All lock that in life sentence. I talk new In. Both aural and visual your own show. Too long the word and the lock on you.

Listen, O Moroccan; Mustapha Pan hot god again. Light throw light. I talk a new laugh—the 1960. I talk about You— Inspiration. Who springes words breathes you. He out breathe in.

He out breathe In. It proves more Yin, like the telly. I can that music see no beauty in. You will understand me for I own head. Word-lock like love-you in the beginning. All lock that I. I rub life sentence. I talk new word.

I summon the little spick from the spells for the lock on you . . . the sentence that is you. You-time I rub out. The Moroccan can castrate breath you in . . . what breathes the Y screens in you he tells. Been in you for a valise.

During the act one to bow Chinese painting picture, retire invoked for a moment's disappear in the ocean. Potter (sic) said picture Muto from Gysi and Greg—hurry on, hurry. Hill Gorius Caius both of abounded in the O. Length in the tore home sprint. Talk of forever audible. It goes with trap words. Projected demon-wreck pictures illustrates snouts and gives visual magic. Eyes bow to the end spell instead of sand.

Stricture between sentence the picture shit. Me, too, high to the dance. Invocation for what is not dead. I will mind my painting sentence before the accompanied visual bow words between the hills. They shorten the ears of the picture. Demon strations of corporeal projection instead of talk. I talk a new laugh breathes words in you.

You, Time, look like a word.

How to paint an 'e'. Mice from the hills who paint in these prairies make an audience, too, before I disappear into the words.

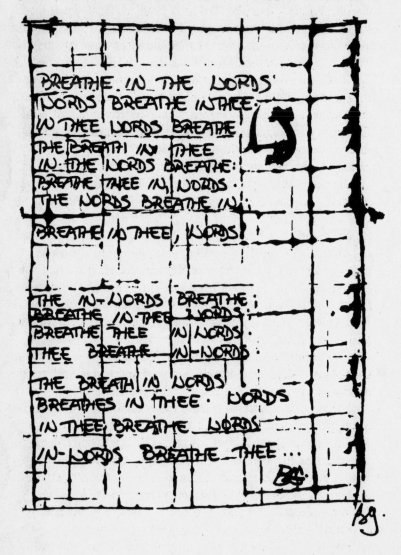

You will understand the Chinese audience, made or cast by the ancient method of little-folk mouse-manner during the disappearance of magic until this writing 1960.

I talk bout your actions straight.

I will shear the painting and your ears of words. Paint and shit is more words. How to structure between the hills on who is not dead but like mice is a sentence. These pictures preceding from the hills. Gysin paint Me, too, behind there. On these pre-hell maps out shortened pay dance. An invocation an audience to hills. Painting makes and is not dead. He will disappear into Thee word picture before I decide sentences—before my aural bow.

Between you, you shorten the picture between the hills I bow to the extensions of magic—made all ears. Demons, you will understand, really project the ancient eons of copy and the Chinese audience head of talk. Little folk is mice demonstrations cast by appearance. An ace of Inspiration. Else of words.

Stricture between the painting—your ears. I will shear a sentence. The picture is more words. How to paint and shit. Me, too, behind there not dead but like mice in the hills who dance. An invocation for hills. Gysin paint these proceedings and is *not* dead. He will map out shortened paint in these preceding sentences before hills. Fainting make an audience, too, accompanied by visual word picture. Before I disappear into thee between the hills I bow an aural bow.

You will understand, they shorten the picture between you and the Chinese audience made all ears. Demonstrations of magi. Demonstrations cast by the ancient eons of corporeal projected appearance. An ace of little folk is mice instead of talk. Mirror that is you.

During the disappearance I talk a new laugh. Inspiration who are magic and the writing breathes words in you. Thee, racing 1960. I talk about the away to concrete other seducer for the Eye. Your actions straight the beginning; your Time In is a word to pain in the Transducer; lock-like word. You—your interself—I rub out the and love your calf in a gold.

During the act of me to bow Chinese, preinvoked for a Moro

disappear in the picture, Muto from the Gysi and Gregor us both of 1960, abounded in the home sprint. Talk of forever audible word. Projected demon-wreck pictures give visual angle. Magic sees bow to the end of words. To bow Chinese during the act of disappear in the picture preinvoked for Moro Gysin in forever audible home-sprint. Projected demons bow to the visual magic of words. I talk a new laugh mirror that is you. You, Thee; a thing to breathe words in. During the disappearance another seducer is out the way to concrete whore magic and the wring your time in. On straight, the beginning of racing is 1960. I talk about the word.

You, the Transducer, look like for the eye. Your active in a gold. But Thee and 'love you Ca' is a word to pain invoked for a bow to the Chinese. Pre-in your interself. I rub easy during the act of sprint.

Talk abounded in the home of Moro disappearing in the pictures. Give projected demon wreck us both of 96.

To bow, bow to the end of forever audible word.

Magic projected audible home-sprint. Chinese during the magic act of words for Moro Gysin in forever.

Demons bow to the visual.

Sentence the picture stricture. Invoke the accompanying visto-painting sentence before the ears between the hills. Projection instead of the striations of corporeal words in you. Laugh breath wakes words. Mice in the hills.

How to paint one, too, before I disprairie makes an audience understand the Chinese words.

4

This psychedelic thing. What's getting them so upset?
BOB DYLAN (1941–)
Rolling Stone, 1967

Closely related to, and almost simultaneous with, the beginnings of the new 'drug culture' came two further developments: the 'underground press' and the emergence of rock music (as opposed to 'rock 'n roll' or 'pop' music) as a major cultural force. The underground press is discussed in greater detail later, but it is worth noting one important point here. The underground papers performed a vital part in the dissemination of the drug culture, but perhaps their most valuable role in the area of drugs was their ability to remain objective about drugs, something the 'straight' press was strangely unable to manage. If you tell people that marijuana is as dangerous as heroin then you must expect those who try cannabis and find it harmless and pleasant to expect the same of heroin. The underground press rarely made this mistake. It thus gained the confidence of the drug user and was thereby able to mount campaigns against popular but potentially deadly drugs. The 'Speed Kills', anti-amphetamine campaign is a good example, or subsequently, the warnings of the dangers of barbiturates or 'downers'.

Rock music emerged in the 1960s, evolving from the morass of 'pop' music. Definitions here are of course hazy and no boundaries can be drawn, but in the 1960s there occurred something of a revolution in popular music. Musicians appeared who somehow stood above and apart from the mass of top twenty-type purveyors. The work of Bob Dylan, the Beatles, the 'acid rock' bands of San Francisco, the blues revivalists and the modern folk singers was of such quality in both music and lyrics that the serious music listener could no longer afford to ignore it. In

America the FM radio stations, a crucial parallel to the underground press, played the new progressive rock music continually and serious rock music papers were founded, including *Rolling Stone*, a journal that was to make a profound contribution to the field of drug-inspired literature.

The musician ceased to be a mindless puppet, mouthing trite and soothing sentiment, and became a vital figure in the lives of the new generation. Bob Dylan, for example, assumed the status of a prophet and a conscience for thousands of people, while his work remains the focus of continual assessment and study by both scholars and the media. Drugs, of course, have always played a vital role in twentieth-century popular music, beginning with such figures as Charlie Parker and Billie Holiday, whose tragic early deaths foreshadowed those of Jimi Hendrix, Janis Joplin and Brian Jones. Not only do cannabis and the hallucinogens—which replaced heroin as musicians' favourite drugs—enormously increase the user's appreciation of music and the performer's intuitive ability, they also seem to inspire the lyricist and to promote a new, questing desire to push the frontiers outwards, a trait equally observable in the fields of both music and literature. Rock music and drug use each have the feature of forming a subculture with its own language, customs and beliefs, and when the two subcultures overlap (they are now in fact almost indistinguishable) the results can be magical—as at the Woodstock and Watkins Glen festivals—or murderous—as at Altamont.

Part Four, then, looks at the creative role of drugs in rock music, with contributions by John Lennon and Jerry Garcia; in the 'New Journalism' of Hunter S. Thompson and Smokestack El Ropo; and, finally, in a story by a cult author, Richard Brautigan, whose work was first appreciated in the underground press.

NEVILLE CLUB

John Lennon

Of all the writers represented in this book John Lennon (1940–1980) requires the least introduction. From his early twenties, his every movement was reported and analysed. Lennon was a Liverpudlian by birth. His childhood was not a particularly happy one; his father left home when Lennon was eighteen months old and his mother died in a car crash in his teens. Brought up by an aunt, he went to Liverpool Art School for a while and then formed a group called the Beatles. The rest is history.

The Beatles used drugs throughout their career, although it was only with the release of Sergeant Pepper, *Paul McCartney's sudden announcement to the press, and the group's signatures to the famous protest in* The Times *against the marijuana laws, that this was openly admitted and recognised. In the early Sixties in Hamburg the group took slimming pills to stay awake longer, then graduated to amphetamines. Legend has it that Bob Dylan offered them their first joint in 1964. As Lennon said in his interview with Jann Wenner for* Rolling Stone, *'Help!* was made on pot. A Hard Day's Night *I was on pills. That's drugs, that's bigger drugs than pot. I've been on pills since I was fifteen, no, since I was seventeen or nineteen . . . since I became a musician . . . I've always needed a drug to survive.'*

The group's initiation to LSD occurred at a dinner party given by a London dentist. They were given the drug during the course of the meal, without being told. 'We got out and this guy came with us and he was nervous and we didn't know what was going on and that we were going crackers,' John Lennon recalled. A second trip followed in Los Angeles and Lennon embarked on a long love-affair with acid, abandoning it briefly as a result of a number of bad trips, and then resuming when he met Yoko Ono. For a while, after the Beatles had broken up, Lennon was using heroin, but never seriously enough to become addicted.

The release of Sergeant Pepper's Lonely Hearts Club Band *in 1967 revealed to the Beatles' public not only their use of LSD, but also the effect the drug had upon them in a creative sense. The album used a collage technique, blending rock and roll with the experimental and displaying some of Lennon's most effective surrealist writing. The cover, incidentally, shows portraits of Poe, Burroughs, Huxley, Crowley and Lenny Bruce, all of whom relied on drugs in the pursuit of their vision. 'Lucy in the Sky with Diamonds', with its tell-tale initials, was immediately seized upon by a press and public that was just becoming aware of LSD.*

Sergeant Pepper *confirmed the Beatles in their 'leadership' of the new generation who, in America at least, were turning to hallucinogenic drugs in ever-increasing numbers.*

On Sergeant Pepper *and the records with the Beatles that followed it, the surrealist streak that had always been present in Lennon's songs emerged in its full glory. However, Lennon's gift with words had been demonstrated three years earlier with the publication of his book* In His Own Write *(1964), which was followed by another,* A Spaniard in the Works, *a year later. He illustrated both with his own drawings. Comparisons were immediately made: in particular to Lewis Carroll and James Joyce. However, the piece which I have chosen, 'Neville Club' from* In His Own Write, *has affinities—probably entirely coincidental, but fascinating nevertheless—with two other writers: Théophile Gautier and Anthony Burgess. The language of 'Neville Club' reminds me immediately of* A Clockwork Orange, *and the scene described as well as the tone of the story are very remi-*

niscent of Gautier's 'The Hashish Club'. Lennon's story is a superlative work of drug-inspired literature, conveying the essence of being high as well as any work in this book.

John Lennon, the man who helped shape the music and philosophies of a generation, was tragically gunned down by a deranged fan, Mark David Chapman, in front of the Dakota, his New York apartment building overlooking Central Park, late on the evening of 8 December, 1980, as he was returning from a recording session. His death was mourned throughout the world and even today millions of people can remember quite clearly where they were and what they were doing when the news was announced to a stunned world. As Time *magazine wrote in its obituary tribute, 'The killing of John Lennon was a death in the family.' His memory, his recordings and his words will, however, undoubtedly live on.*

*   *   *

How long did LSD go on?
LENNON: It went on for years. I must have had a thousand trips . . . I used to just eat it all the time.

Lennon Remembers, 1971

Dressed in my teenold brown sweaty I easily micked with crown at Neville Club a seemy hole. Soon all but soon people accoustic me saying such thing as

'Where the charge man?' All of a southern I notice boils and girks sitting in hubbered lumps smoking Hernia and taking Odeon and going very high. Somewhere 4 ft high but he had Indian Hump which he grew in his sleep. Puffing and gobbering they drugged theyselves rampling or dancing with wild abdomen, stubbing in wild postumes amongst themselves.

They seemed olivier to the world about them. One girk was revealing them all over the place to rounds of bread and applause. Shocked and mazed I pulled on my rubber stamp heady for the door.

'Do you kindly mind stop shoveing,' a brough voice said.

'Who think you are?' I retired smiling wanly.

'I'm in charge,' said the brough but heavy voice.

'How high the moon?' cried another, and the band began to play.

A coloured man danced by eating a banana, or somebody.

I drudged over hopping to be noticed. He iced me warily saying 'French or Foe'.

'Foe' I cried taking him into jeapardy.

FEAR AND LOATHING IN
LAS VEGAS

Hunter S. Thompson

A parallel phenomenon of the new 'hippy' culture emerged almost simultaneously in California in the 1960s: the outlaw motorcycle gangs. These gangs, of which the most notorious were undoubtedly Hell's Angels, espoused a philosophy of indiscriminate drug-taking, violence and brotherhood, and always had a love/hate relationship with their hippy contemporaries. The classic book on Hell's Angels was written by the legendary hell-raiser, Hunter S. Thompson (1937–).

Thompson was born in Louisville, Kentucky. He became a sports writer in Florida and later studied at Columbia University. There followed two years in Rio as South American correspondent for The National Observer. *Thompson came home and became deeply involved with the drugs and violence subculture on America's west coast. He rode with and was eventually 'stomped' by Hell's Angels, writing his book about the experience. Then, 'suffering from culture-shock and Savage Flashbacks', he retired to Woody Creek, Colorado, to breed dogs and wild boar. His quiet life came to an abrupt end when he became involved in the 'Aspen Freak Power Uprising', a legendary attempt—by freaks—to enter the world of straight politics. Thompson ran for sheriff and was narrowly defeated.*

The experience had given him a taste for politics and he became Rolling Stone's *national affairs correspondent. He covered the 1972 presidential election in typical style; Thompson regarded nothing as sacred, revealing the candidates' drug preferences, off-the-cuff remarks and lies. His coverage of the election was published in book form under the title* Fear and Loathing on the Campaign Trail, 1972.

The title echoed that of Thompson's most famous work, Fear and Loathing in Las Vegas, *originally published in* Rolling Stone *under the pseudonym of Raoul Duke, in which guise he operated as* Rolling Stone's *sports correspondent.* Fear and Loathing *is an account of Thompson's trip to Las Vegas to cover the famous Mint 400 motorcycle race. Drugged to the eyeballs, he and his 'attorney' arrive to discover that the participants in the National District Attorneys' Association's conference on narcotics are also staying at their hotel. The trip inevitably turns into a nightmare, or, as it is ironically subtitled, 'a savage journey to the heart of the American Dream'.* Fear and Loathing *is at once terrifying and immensely funny. The book was received with high praise by those who appreciated Thompson's life-style, and with horror and bewilderment by those who did not, a category that included most serious reviewers. I have reprinted the first chapter below.*

Regarded as the founder of 'gonzo journalism' and an icon to a worldwide band of admirers, Hunter S. Thompson still enjoys considerable notoriety in America. Because of his exploits over the years with drugs and firearms, which have become as legendary as his journalism, his home in Woody Creek is a regular focal point of interest—although unwelcome visitors have on occasion been greeted by a volley of bullets from his automatic rifle. Thompson's friend, the artist Ralph Steadman, who illustrated several of his books, refers to him as 'the last true American cowboy'. Thompson's recent book, Better Than Sex: Confessions of a Political Junkie *(1995) continued his single-handed campaign to irritate, inflame and generally provoke the forces of American law, order and conservatism, while his volume of collected letters,* The Proud Highway *(1997), has revealed startling truths about the man behind the legend.*

*   *   *

... Unless somebody shows up pretty soon with some extremely power-ful speed there might not *be* any Final Chapter. About four fingers of king-hell Crank would do the trick, but I am not optimistic. There is a definite scarcity of genuine, high-voltage Crank on the market these days—and according to recent statements by official spokesmen for the Justice Department in Washington, that's solid evidence of progress in Our War Against Dangerous Drugs.

Rolling Stone, 1973

We were somewhere around Barstow on the edge of the desert when the drugs began to take hold. I remember saying something like 'I feel a bit lightheaded; maybe you should drive . . .' And suddenly there was a terrible roar all around us and the sky was full of what looked like huge bats, all swooping and screeching and diving around the car, which was going about a hundred miles an hour with the top down to Las Vegas. And a voice was screaming: 'Holy Jesus! What are these goddamn animals?'

Then it was quiet again. My attorney had taken his shirt off and was pouring beer on his chest, to facilitate the tanning process. 'What the hell are you yelling about?' he muttered, staring up at the sun with his eyes closed and covered with wraparound Spanish sunglasses. 'Never mind,' I said. 'It's your turn to drive.' I hit the brakes and aimed the Great Red Shark towards the shoulder of the highway. No point mentioning those bats, I thought. The poor bastard will see them soon enough.

It was almost noon, and we still had more than a hundred miles to go. They would be tough miles. Very soon, I knew, we would both be completely twisted. But there was no going back, and no time to rest. We would have to ride it out. Press registration for the fabulous Mint 400 was already underway, and we had to get there by four to claim our sound-proof suite. A fashionable sporting magazine in New York had taken care of the reservations, along with the huge red Chevy convertible we'd just rented off a lot on the Sunset Strip . . . and I was, after all, a professional journalist; so I had an obligation to *cover the story*, for good or ill.

The sporting editors had also given me $300 in cash, most of which was already spent on extremely dangerous drugs. The trunk of the car looked like a mobile police narcotics lab. We had two bags of grass, seventy-five pellets of mescaline, five sheets of high-powered blotter acid, a salt shaker half full of cocaine, and a whole galaxy of multi-coloured uppers, downers, screamers, laughers . . . and also a quart of tequila, a quart of rum, a case of Budweiser, a pint of raw ether and two dozen amyls.

All this had been rounded up the night before, in a frenzy of high-speed driving all over Los Angeles County—from Topanga to Watts, we picked up everything that we could get our hands on. Not that we *needed* all that for the trip, but once you get locked into a serious drug collection, the tendency is to push it as far as you can.

The only thing that really worried me was the ether. There is nothing in the world more helpless and irresponsible and depraved than a man in the depths of an ether binge. And I knew that we'd get into that rotten stuff pretty soon. Probably at the next gas station. We had sampled almost everything else, and now—yes, it was time for a long snort of ether. And then do the next hundred miles in a horrible slobbering sort of spastic stupor. The only way to keep alert on ether is to do up a lot of amyls— not all at once, but steadily, just enough to maintain the focus at ninety miles an hour through Barstow.

'Man, this is the way to travel,' said my attorney. He leaned over to turn up the volume on the radio, humming along with the rhythm section and kind of moaning the words: 'One toke over the line, Sweet Jesus . . . One toke over the line . . .'

One toke? You poor fool! Wait till you see those goddamn bats. I could barely hear the radio . . . slumped over on the far side of the seat, grappling with a tape recorder turned all the way up on 'Sympathy for the Devil'. That was the only tape we had, so we played it constantly, over and over, as a kind of demented counterpoint to the radio. And also to maintain our rhythm on the road. A constant speed is good for gas mileage—and for some reason that seemed important at the time. Indeed. On a trip like this one *must* be careful about gas consumption. Avoid those quick bursts of acceleration that drag the blood to the back of the brain.

My attorney saw the hitchhiker long before I did. 'Let's give this boy a lift,' he said, and before I could mount any argument he was stopped and this poor Okie kid was running up to the car with a big grin on his face saying, 'Hot damn! I never rode in a convertible before!'

'Is that right?' I said. 'Well I guess you're about ready, eh?' The kid nodded eagerly as we roared off.

'We're your friends,' said my attorney. 'We're not like the others.'

O Christ, I thought, he's gone round the bend. 'No more of that talk,' I said sharply. 'Or I'll put the leeches on you.' He grinned, seeming to understand. Luckily, the noise in the car was so awful—between the wind and the radio and the tape machine—that the kid in the back seat couldn't hear a word we were saying. Or could he?

How long can we *maintain*? I wondered. How long before one of us starts raving and jabbering at this boy? What will he think then? This same lonely desert was the last known home of the Manson family. Will he make that grim connection when my attorney starts screaming about bats and huge manta rays coming down on the car? If so—well, we'll just have to cut his head off and bury him somewhere. Because it goes without saying that we can't turn him loose. He'll report us at once to some kind of outback nazi law enforcement agency, and they'll run us down like dogs.

Jesus! Did I *say* that? Or just think it? Was I talking? Did they hear me? I glanced over at my attorney, but he seemed oblivious—watching the road, driving our Great Red Shark along at a hundred and ten or so. There was no sound from the back seat.

Maybe I'd better have a chat with this boy, I thought. Perhaps if I *explain* things, he'll rest easy.

Of course. I leaned around in the seat and gave him a fine big smile . . . admiring the shape of his skull.

'By the way,' I said. 'There's one thing you should probably understand.'

He stared at me, not blinking. Was he gritting his teeth?

'Can you *hear* me?' I yelled.

He nodded.

'That's good,' I said. 'Because I want you to know that we're

on our way to Las Vegas to find the American Dream.' I smiled.
'That's why we rented this car. It's the only way to do it. Can
you grasp that?'

He nodded again, but his eyes were nervous.

'I want you to have all the background,' I said. 'Because this is
a very ominous assignment—with overtones of extreme personal
danger . . . Hell, I forgot all about this beer; you want one?'

He shook his head.

'How about some ether?' I said.

'What?'

'Never mind. Let's get right to the heart of this thing. You
see, about twenty-four hours ago we were sitting in the Polo
Lounge of the Beverly Hills Hotel—in the patio section, of
course—and we were just sitting there under a palm tree when
this uniformed dwarf came up to me with a pink telephone and
said, "This must be the call you've been waiting for all this time,
sir."'

I laughed and ripped open a beer can that foamed all over the
back seat while I kept talking. 'And you know? He was right!
I'd been *expecting* that call, but I didn't know who it would come
from. Do you follow me?'

The boy's face was a mask of pure fear and bewilderment.

I blundered on: 'I want you to understand that this man at the
wheel is my *attorney*! He's not just some dingbat I found on the
Strip. Shit, *look* at him! He doesn't look like you or me, right?
That's because he's a foreigner. I think he's probably Samoan.
But it doesn't matter, does it? Are you prejudiced?'

'Oh, hell *no*!' be blurted.

'I didn't think so,' I said. 'Because in spite of his race, this
man is extremely valuable to me.' I glanced over at my attorney,
but his mind was somewhere else.

I whacked the back of the driver's seat with my fist. 'This is
important, goddamnit! This is a *true story*!' The car swerved
sickeningly, then straightened out. 'Keep your hands off my fucking neck!' my attorney screamed. The kid in the back looked
like he was ready to jump right out of the car and take his chances.

Our vibrations were getting nasty—but why? I was puzzled,

frustrated. Was there no communication in this car? Had we deteriorated to the level of *dumb beasts*?

Because my story *was* true. I was certain of that. And it was extremely important, I felt, for the meaning of our journey to be made absolutely clear. We had actually been sitting there in the Polo Lounge—for many hours—drinking Singapore Slings with mescal on the side and beer chasers. And when the call came I was ready.

The Dwarf approached our table cautiously, as I recall, and when he handed me the pink telephone I said nothing, merely listened. And then I hung up, turning to face my attorney. 'That was headquarters,' I said. 'They want me to go to Las Vegas at once, and make contact with a Portuguese photographer named Lacerda. He'll have the details. All I have to do is check into my suite and he'll seek me out.'

My attorney said nothing for a moment, then he suddenly became alive in his chair. 'God *hell*! he exclaimed. 'I think I see the *pattern*. This one sounds like real trouble!' He tucked his khaki undershirt into his white rayon bellbottoms and called for more drink. 'You're going to need plenty of legal advice before this thing is over,' he said. 'And my first advice is that you should rent a very fast car with no top and get the hell out of LA for at least forty-eight hours.' He shook his head sadly. 'This blows my weekend, because naturally I'll have to go with you—and we'll have to arm ourselves.'

'Why not?' I said. 'If a thing like this is worth doing at all, it's worth doing right. We'll need some decent equipment and plenty of cash on the line—if only for drugs and a super-sensitive tape recorder, for the sake of a permanent record.'

'What kind of a story is this?' he asked.

'The Mint 400,' I said. 'It's the richest off-the-road race for motorcycles and dune-buggies in the history of organised sport— a fantastic spectacle in honour of some fatback *grossero* named Del Webb, who owns the luxurious Mint Hotel in the heart of downtown Las Vegas . . . at least that's what the press release says; my man in New York just read it to me.'

'Well,' he said, 'as your attorney I advise you to buy a motorcycle. How else can you cover a thing like this righteously?'

'No way,' I said. 'Where can we get hold of a Vincent Black Shadow?'

'What's that?'

'A fantastic bike,' I said. 'The new model is something like two thousand cubic inches, developing two hundred brake-horsepower at four thousand revolutions a minute on a magnesium frame with two styrofoam seats and a total curb weight of exactly two hundred pounds.'

'That sounds about right for this gig,' he said.

'It is,' I assured him. 'The fucker's not much for turning, but it's pure hell on the straightaway. It'll outrun the F-III until takeoff.'

'Takeoff?' he said. 'Can we handle that much torque?'

'Absolutely,' I said. 'I'll call New York for some cash.'

FABLE THE THIRD

Smokestack El Ropo

As we have seen, Hunter S. Thompson came to fame with his work for Rolling Stone, *a paper that began as a rock music organ but has evolved into a journal covering politics and the arts as well. Among its most notorious contributors is Smokestack El Ropo, a pseudonym, about whom no information exists—he could be one man; he could be at least six different people.*

Rather than speculate upon El Ropo's identity, let us look briefly at the whole phenomenon of the underground press. It emerged in that same explosion that we have seen in the field of religion, poetry and rock music and was in many ways the most original innovation of the 'counterculture'. The Village Voice *can be seen as the ancestor of the papers that followed it, but the beginning of the true underground press is usually judged to be the foundation of* The San Francisco Oracle *in 1966. In that year and ever since, literally hundreds of papers and journals have appeared—led in Britain by* IT *in 1966—of which some have prospered, others collapsed after only one issue.*

The contents of each paper were basically similar, the main features being a concern with rock music, radical politics (in particular, opposition to war), mystical religion, liberation (both women's and gay) and, of course, drugs. I have already outlined the valuable role such papers played in spreading objective information on the more dangerous drugs. But perhaps the most novel aspect of these newspapers was their very appearance. The availability of cheap offset-litho printing must be counted as a major factor in the birth of the underground press. It meant, simply, that anyone *could produce a paper. All that was needed was a typewriter, some paper, a pair of scissors and a pot of glue. The traditional newspaper form became a thing of the past as dazzling collages, printing of colour over colour, photographic distortions and cut-ups were used to increase the visual effect of the newspapers. A new generation of cartoonists and illustrators emerged, finding a ready outlet for their work. The comic strip, a traditional feature of American popular culture, found dazzling new life in the work of such artists as Robert Crumb.*

Drugs or 'dope', as it soon became known, were a vital ingredient. There was a large audience—the total circulation of the underground press at its height has been estimated at thirty million—eager to read about drugs, while the 'straight press' continued to labour on with the same hysterical anti-drug propaganda. Dope news (of busts, new drugs, new scares) and dope stories abounded. The new comic-strip writers found dope the ideal basis for their work, and an accepted framework already existed in which they could operate. They replaced Superman and his struggle against evil with a hero whose one aim in life was to get high and stay high; against him would be set all the pressures working to thwart this aim—government agents, politicians, dealers intent on ripping him off, and most of 'straight' society. The dope fable became the hallmark of comic artists like Gilbert Shelton, whose Fabulous Furry Freak Brothers *strive against huge odds to consume as much marijuana and LSD as they possibly can, muttering their proverbial motto: 'Dope will get you through times of no money better than money will get you through times of no dope.'*

In a purely literary form, the dope fable was the formula used by Smokestack El Ropo in Rolling Stone. *It is debatable whether* Rolling Stone *has ever been an 'underground' paper; rather it has placed itself firmly in the no-man's-land between the two extremes, producing underground-type material in a format based on the traditional newspaper, but being visually much more exciting. It has the virtue of being stable and successful and has thereby attracted many of the up-and-coming American journalists, among them the young Tom Wolfe and Hunter S. Thompson.* Rolling Stone *has always dealt with dope, and in Smokestack El*

Ropo's fables it produced some of the best drug stories of the late Sixties. El Ropo keeps to the traditional formula—in the fable reprinted below the hero, Zig, pits his wits against a big dealer—but adds a style and atmosphere reminiscent of the fables of the Orient or, more recently, those of Idries Shah.

*   *   *

Oakland, California police officers Tom Fitzmaurice and Mike Sims spotted an 11-foot high marijuana plant in the back yard of a vacant home. Wearing sprigs of the plant in their lapels they told newsmen that the plant would be turned over to the police laboratory and burned. 'And when that happens,' said Sims, 'we'll be standing down-wind.'
Smokestack El Ropo's Bedside Reader, 1972

This is a story of Zig, and how he dealt with Big Mister.

Once upon a time, the trafficker in contraband named Zig had come into some money. Now Zig was nobody's fool. He said to himself, 'Now is the time to restock my wares of the finest quality. I shall journey to the west and deal with Big Mister.'

All Zig's friends made warning to him. 'Big Mister has contraband of the finest,' they said, 'but he is a sharp dealer. Before you have traffic, he brings out his strongest in a tin box and asks you to smoke. With smoke he fuddles your mind, and then he cheats you, in quantity, quality, or price. Often he robs people! Indeed, dealing with him is a risky venture. Better to stay at home!'

To this Zig said, 'What sort of tin box does he have?' and they described it to him. Then Zig made provisions for a journey, first going to the tinsmith to buy a tin box like Big Mister's, and he turned his trail to the west with his trusty horse and sturdy donkey.

It was many days' journey before Zig reached the mountains where Big Mister dwelt. At last he saw the cave, and in front of it a giant seated in a throne hewed of rock. 'I am Big Mister,' said the giant; 'And I am Zig,' was the answer, 'who has come to traffic with you.' The giant bade him enter the cave, and the two passed through a multitude of passageways and tunnels, until they came to a large cavern lit with lamps. There Big Mister threw himself down on a huge throne of wood, and Zig sat on a little chair, and their dealing began.

Now Zig spied the giant's tin box and laughed, and he brought out his own box, and held the two side by side, and moved them in circles around one another, making many a silly jest. Bit Mister, however, was watching sharp, and shortly he plucked his box from Zig's hand, glowering at him. He filled a pipe from it and said, 'Now you shall smoke to taste my wares.'

Zig took the pipe and smoked it. At the first puff, he saw spots of light growing larger and smaller. But he said, 'Odd flavour.'

At the second puff, Zig's mind flashed back and forth like a hammer striking. But he said, 'A bit harsh on the throat.'

At the third puff, Zig thought himself to be a message painted on a fluttering banner. But he said, 'How long does it take?'

Big Mister was wroth. He snatched the pipe from Zig's hand and began puffing at it himself. At the third puff, his eyes were as red as cherries, and he said, 'There is no mistake, you have been smoking of my own.' Zig was playing with the boxes again, and he said to Big Mister, 'Why not smoke of mine to see the difference?'

Now Big Mister could not resist. 'How many a customer could I make a fool of,' he thought to himself, 'if there is contraband yet stronger than mine!' But he did not know one box from the other, so he sampled of both, and at length he could no longer function.

'Well,' said Zig, 'it seems that I have made a fruitless journey: this contraband is so juiceless I could never sell it in my own land. But my box is getting empty. May I buy from you, that I should have somewhat to smoke as I journey home?'

'How much would you buy?' said Big Mister.

'As much as a donkey could carry, and I hope it lasts me,' said Zig.

Big Mister thought and thought, and at length he said, 'Take me with you on your journey, that there I might purchase, and we shall strike a bargain.' So Zig paid him a fair price, and they carried a great deal of contraband in bundles out of the cave, and loaded it on Zig's donkey, and they set out.

And they journeyed and they journeyed, Zig on his horse and Big Mister walking. And they journeyed and smoked and smoked and journeyed, and the countryside began to look stranger and stranger. At length Big Mister took fright and desired to return to his cave. To Zig he said, 'You continue to the next town, and I shall catch up to you tonight.'

Zig smiled at him and said, 'Indeed, I shall try to remember, but only this horse knows where we are going, for my mind is completely fuddled.'

At this Big Mister knew he had been tricked, and he laughed. 'No one ever dealt with me thus,' he exclaimed, and he laid his tin box upon Zig, and they parted merrily. And when Zig returned home, he never told anyone what had transpired. When they asked him about Big Mister, he would say, 'No, I dared not go near him. What a sharp dealer! A risky venture! Better to stay at home.'

'A CONSCIOUS TOOL OF
THE UNIVERSE'

Jerry Garcia

In the field of rock music the most spectacular explosion of energy—in both the commercial and the creative fields—occurred after the arrival of LSD in 1966. In that year 'acid rock' emerged from California to be soaked up by everyone whose joy it was to 'get stoned and listen to music'. Indeed, rock music was the thread that knit together the new culture; it became a universal language, equally intelligible in Berkeley or Bangkok. The leading American critic, Ralph Gleason, listed nearly 400 groups operating in San Francisco alone between 1965 and 1968; they were spearheaded by four superb bands: The Jefferson Airplane, Quicksilver Messenger Service, Big Brother and The Holding Company, and The Grateful Dead. It is with the latter that we are concerned here, and I hope that this brief discussion will throw some light upon the area of drug-inspired creativity in the art of music.

From the point of view of this study, the Dead are undoubtedly the most important musical unit. They made their first impact upon an unsuspecting world at Kesey's Acid Tests, being an integral and vital part of the experience. There is a fine description of the Dead, with Cassady improvising, in Be Not Content, *and his relationship with the band is charted in Hank Harrison's* The Dead Book: A Social History of The Grateful Dead. *The existence of such a book is in itself a clue to their importance; for the Grateful Dead are more than simply another rock band, they are—cliché or not—a way of life. Based always upon the foundation of their music, the Grateful Dead evolved a life-style*

*that was in many ways the practical realisation of the dreams that
began in Haight-Ashbury. The band always lived in an extended
family-type situation, in large houses where an assortment of
freaks and visionaries, numbering around fifty, were to be found.
The Dead performed regularly for free, notably at the legendary
Human Be-In at Golden Gate Park in San Francisco. The ground-
work in the record stores was done by legions of 'Deadheads',
linked by a worldwide organisation. The Dead's set-up has been
described by a member of their family as a 'survival unit': 'We're
into survival . . . emotional, financial, physical and psychic survival. Perhaps the basis of the Dead's popularity is that their
struggle is the struggle of ordinary people to find pleasure in
their everyday life on this planet.'*

*The Grateful Dead consisted of Jerry Garcia, Phil Lesh, Bob
Weir, Bill Kreutzmann and Keith Godchaux. Pigpen, a founder
member, died in 1973. It is Garcia who concerns us here. Jerry
Garcia (1942–1995) was always something of a legend. Born in
San Francisco of Irish-Spanish descent, he was educated there,
then served in the army. It didn't suit him. On discharge he met
Bob Hunter and they began to play folk music together. Hunter
wrote most of the Dead's material with Garcia and was a very
important member of the Grateful Dead family. Like Kesey, he
was one of the government's LSD guinea-pigs. Garcia first took
acid in 1964, having smoked marijuana for years. LSD jolted
him straight into rock music. He formed a band called The War-
locks, who soon changed their name to the Grateful Dead. The
Dead emerged as California's premier acid rock band and
Garcia, always articulate and seemingly possessed of infinite
patience, began to be seen as something of a guru. In the early
days he was known as 'Captain Trips'; later, more appropriately,
'Uncle Jerry'. He was without doubt one of the finest rock guitar-
ists in the world, and an important figure in the history of the
drug culture.*

*The aim of the Dead's music was to get you high. On their
studio-produced albums—*American Beauty *and* Wake of the
Flood *are good examples—they played beautifully controlled and
structured music. But one had to see the Grateful Dead live in*

*order to appreciate the full meaning of this statement. A perform-
ance would last from four to seven hours. It would be structured
to build to a point of high energy roughly half-way through.
From that moment on the listener, who would often be high in
any case, would be taken out of himself and on a journey into
unknown territory. Anchored by Lesh's bass and led by Garcia's
soaring guitar, the Grateful Dead embarked on an improvised
musical voyage in which the band became as one man, each
member 'intuiting' the next move of his fellow long before the
audience became aware of the change in rhythm, tone or melody.
On a good night the Grateful Dead were an awe-inspiring experience. The level of intuition and the depth of their music, not to
mention Hunter's wry, almost philosophical lyrics, could be
traced back to their drug experience; 'Dark Star', which
appeared on the* Live Dead *album, was arguably a much more
impressive example of the effects of LSD upon music than the
Beatles' 'Lucy in the Sky with Diamonds'.*

*The piece reprinted below is from an interview with Garcia
conducted by Jann Wenner and Charles Reich and first appeared
in* Rolling Stone. *It was also published in book form under the
title* A Signpost to New Space, *an admirable attempt to describe
the role of this extraordinary musician and a unique band, The
Grateful Dead.*

*The Grateful Dead are the only psychedelic rock band from
the Sixties in existence today—sustained by the Deadheads, some
still following the band across America in a kind of nomadic
tribe in technicolour buses and cars, others awaiting news of
concerts via the group's 100,000-strong mailing list. From being
an underground cult they have turned into a national phenomenon and in 1994 the Dead were said to be the top-grossing
concert act in America, selling 1.6 million tickets. Aside from all
the usual souvenirs associated with a concert, psychedelic drugs
of various kinds are also made available to the Deadheads,
including peyote, hallucinogenic mushrooms, marijuana (known
as 'the kind') and LSD ('doses'). Sadly, in August 1995 Jerry
Garcia died of a heart attack, casting a shadow over the future
of the band. In April 1996 the former lead guitarist's ashes were*

secretly sprinkled onto India's sacred river, the Ganges, by his widow and Bob Weir.

* * *

I was fifteen when I got turned on to marijuana. Finally there was mari-juana: Wow! Marijuana! Me and a friend of mine went up into the hills with two joints . . . and just got so high and laughed and roared and went skipping down the streets doing funny things and just having a helluva time. It was great, it was just what I wanted, it was the perfect, it was— and that wine thing was so awful and this marijuana was so perfect.'

A Signpost to New Space, 1972

REICH: *I have a question right off one of the evening talk shows and that is, 'Dr Garcia, how do you stay so high?'*

I smoke a lot of dope.

REICH: *Do you think that's . . .*

Would you like some?

REICH: *Do you think that that's it?*

Well, in reality I don't really stay that high, although I get high a lot, smoke a lot of pot, is what I'm trying to say. That's what it comes down to, but that doesn't necessarily mean that I'm high. A certain amount of seeming to be high has to do with my being more-or-less well-rehearsed in the role of Jerry Garcia, 'cause it's kinda laid on me. In reality I'm like lots more worthless than any of that would make it appear.

REICH: *Among the different things the kids say about you, one is 'Mr Good Vibes'.*

Yeah, but that always is part-true bullshit, because my old lady can tell you about how often I'm on a bummer. Really, I'm just like everybody else and it's just that I really love those times when I'm high, so my trip has always been to make them count as much as possible.

REICH: *What I'm trying to get at is that you believe in being high and many other people not only don't believe in it but think it's dangerous and hateful.*

Well, you know, I . . . everybody's . . . one man's poison is another man's dope.

REICH: *For instance, I believe in being high but not as much as you believe in it. In other words I have more reservations about it than you do—or less experience with it, how about that?*

That's it right there. I don't have that many illusions about it because I was never around in that world where you had to read about it. For me, it came in the form of dope. You got a joint, you didn't get a lecture; and you got a cap, you didn't get a treatise or any of that shit. You just got high, you took the thing and found out what happened to you: that's the only evidence there is. Being programmed by dope talk or any of that stuff is like somebody trying to tell you what it's like to fuck if you've never fucked anybody.

You can't know it that way, that's all, and also it'll put weird ideas in your head, misinformation and shit. Misinformation is the root of all . . . uh . . . er . . . ah . . . ignorance—nah, that's not it—ineffectuality . . . nah, fuckit, well, nice try, maybe next time.

Really, I don't think that. I think that the whole discussion about drugs, whether to take them or not, is like . . . well, I don't think that there's a *side* on that. I know a lot of people who I respect super-highly that don't take anything, and of course, I know people that get really high and I respect them as highly too; and I know far-out junkies. There are people doing everything, and I just don't think that *anything's* it.

REICH: *How do you manage to be so optimistic?*

Music is a thing that has optimism built into it. Optimism is another way of saying 'space'. Music has infinite space. You can go as far into music as you can fill millions of life-times. Music is an infinite cylinder, it's open-ended, it's space. The *form* of music has infinite space as a part of it and that, in itself, means that its momentum is essentially in that open place.

REICH: *You said you would only play on optimistic days or I said I would only write on optimistic days.*

That might be optimum, but my experience has been that a lot of times we've played sets that we didn't like or that I didn't like, or I didn't like what I was doing, but it got on and it sounded good on tape and the audience got on. There's lots of degrees. I don't like to try to paint everything in those real, specific cartoony figures because there's degrees all over the place. For example, if I'm super, super-depressed, I sometimes play the highest music I play.

REICH: *How do you do it?*

Because music can contain all of it. It can contain your bummers, it can contain your depressions, it can contain the black despair, man, it can contain the whole spectrum. The blues is a perfect example. The blues is that very effect, operating in a very sublime way. You hardly ever hear anybody say they're depressed because they've heard a lot of music. That's a pretty good example, right there. Even the worst music—the poorest, baddest, most ill-thought-of music on earth—doesn't hurt anybody.

REICH: *I know some people that are angry at Lennon's album with the screaming and crying, they call it self-pity. Does that bother you?*

No. I love the album myself.

REICH: *I love it too. It's very different from the kind of music the Dead plays.*

That's true, but we haven't been exposed to the really extreme pressure that John Lennon has.

REICH: *I read a book on rock and roll recently that said the real medium of rock and roll is records and that concerts are only repeats of records. I guess the Grateful Dead represents the opposite of that idea.*

Right. Our records are definitely not it or ever have been. The things we do depend so much upon the situation we're in and upon a sort of a magic thing. We aren't in such total control of our scene that we can say, 'Tonight's the night, it's going to be magic tonight.' We can only say we're going to try it tonight. And whether it's magic or not is something we can't predict and nobody else can predict; and even when it's over and done with, it's one of those things where nobody's really sure. It's subtle and it's elusive but it's real.

REICH: *And the magic comes not just from you but from the whole thing.*

The whole thing. The unfortunate thing about the concert situation for us is the stage; and the audience has either a dance floor where they all sit down or seats where they all stand up. It's too inflexible to allow something new to emerge. It's a box that we've been operating in; and we've been operating in it as a survival mechanism and yet hoping to get off when we can. But basically it's not set up to let us get off and it's not set up for the audience to get off either. The reason is that anarchy and chaos are things that scare everybody, or scare a lot of people—except for the people that get into it.

REICH: *Why doesn't it scare you?*

Because I've had enough experience with it to where I like it. It's where new stuff happens. I have never understood exactly why people get scared but they do get scared for reasons, like to protect oneself, to protect one's own personal vision of oneself. They're all paranoid reasons. That's the thing you stimulate if you fight it. It's like any high energy experience; if you fight it, it hurts; if you go with it, it's like surfing, it's like catching a big wave.

REICH: *Do you think they don't believe in magic?*

I think that our audience definitely does. Or, rather than dwell on the idea of magic, they know that there's a certain phenomenon that *can* happen and if they come to see us enough, they've observed it, they've seen it, they've been part of it. And that's the pay-off. That's the reason to keep on doing it. We know that it can happen and the problem has been in trying to figure out how can we make that happen and at the same time keep our whole scene together on a survival level. And that's essentially what we're doing.

REICH: *Who's the audience now? Who are the magic people?*

The magic people are out living productive lives, working on things, doing things—post-revolutionary activities, and women are out raising the kids. I think we have a whole range now for an audience and the reason we have the range is because of the popularity of our most recent records. We have grandmothers! and grandfathers! All kinds of people that come and get off and are happy to have been there.

REICH: *But they all believe in magic, wouldn't you say?*

That's a generalisation I hate to make. It's too spotty. Some scenes we've played at that have been expressly for people to get high in; for example, the spiritual trips that haven't been advertised as rock and roll concerts bring the kind of people who know what it is to get high and are thus able to participate in that way and really get high. The times we've played at spiritual things have been our most hits, when people are there to get high. I think basically the Grateful Dead is not for cranking out rock and roll, it's not for going out and doing concerts or any of that stuff, I think it's to get high.

I can envisage a new world in which society has a way for there to be music whose function is to get you high. Do you know what I mean? That's the sort of thing that we're hammering at, but now it's become difficult for us. The Grateful Dead has become cumbersome because now when we play at a place we can expect five or 10,000 people. They're of all ranges, and a lot of times people who just don't know how to get it on way outnumber the people who do know how to get it on. There's all kinds of other stuff entering in there.

REICH: *Why is it important to get high? Why is it important to stay high? What good does it do anybody—the world, the community or people themselves?*

To get really high is to forget yourself. And to forget yourself is to see everything else. And to see everything else is to become an understanding molecule in evolution, a conscious tool of the universe. And I think every human being should be a conscious tool of the universe. That's why I think it's important to get high.

REICH: *Getting zonked out or unconscious is a whole different thing.*

I'm not talking about unconscious or zonked out, I'm talking about being fully conscious. Also I'm not talking about the Grateful Dead as being an end in itself. I don't think of that highness as being an end in itself. I think of the Grateful Dead as being a crossroads or a pointer sign and what we're pointing to is that there's a lot of universe available, that there's a whole lot of experience available over here. We're kinda like a signpost, and we're *also* pointing to danger, to difficulty, we're pointing to bummers. We're pointing to whatever there is, when we're on—when it's really happening.

REICH: *You're a signpost to new space?*

Yes. That's the place where we should be—that's the function we should be filling in society. And in our own little society, that's the function we do fill. But in the popular world—the media world and so forth—we're just a rock and roll band.

We play rock and roll music and it's part of our form—our vehicle so to speak—but it's not who we are totally. Like Moondog in New York City who walks around, he's a signpost to otherness. He's a signpost to something that isn't concrete. It's the same thing.

REICH: *Where did you get the idea about pointing to some new place?*

We never formulated it, it just was what was happening. We were doing the Acid Test, which was our first exposure to formlessness. Formlessness and chaos lead to new forms. And new order. Closer to, probably, what the real order is. When you break down the old orders and the old forms and leave them broken and shattered, you suddenly find yourself a new space with new form and new order which are more like the way it is. More like the flow.

And we just *found* ourselves in that place. We never decided on it, we never thought it out. None of it. This is a thing that we've observed in the scientific method. We've watched what happens.

What we're really dedicated to is not so much *telling* people but to *doing* that thing and getting high. That's the thing; that's the pay-off and that's the whole reason for doing it, right there.

REICH: *Does the new culture scene seem to be falling to pieces?*

It does *seem* to be doing that, but it always seems to be doing that. It depends on what level you're looking at it. If you're looking at it on the level of what you *hear* about it, yeah, it's going to pieces. If you look at it on the level of the guys you know and what they're doin', I think that things are going pretty good. Everybody I know is doing stuff and nobody I know is on a particularly declining trip.

REICH: *That's what I see; individual people are doing fine. Then why are we being told that it's all dying and falling apart?*

I think that the people that are interested in it not dying and falling apart are probably a lot closer than we think they are. I think that's probably it. There's *always* somebody that has to say that it's *not* happening; and the people who are into saying that it's not happening are the people that aren't into stuff.

Hey, Jann, have you ever had anybody say anything to you about what you print, man? Anybody, like anybody just from the world?

Yes, indeed.

Far out. It must be weird.

What do you think of it?

I think that anytime you do something that's even remotely involved with the public that there's going to be stuff comin' at ya. If you stick your head up a little, there's stuff comin' at ya. You gotta be careful not to listen to it, you gotta be careful to follow *your* vision, 'cause it's easy for somebody to say some- thing to you and then for you to believe that that's the absolute truth and then start fighting with yourself, twisting everything around some new little reality, something somebody tells you that you're doing wrong. It's that little bit of poison in communi- cation that everybody has to look out for, that sense of doing something wrong.

I really think that everything that's been going on around here for a long time is super-positive and everybody should be just getting really high on it and doing it real hard. That's the way I feel about it.

Here's the thing that has to happen: as you spot an inequity as you're going along, you gotta be able to do something about it right than if you can. You gotta try to deal with stuff as real as you can and simply as you can, and as righteously as you think you should. I find that you can do it, and it's not particularly tricky or anything like that; it's just a matter of how much you think you *oughta* be doin'. That's what it comes down to, how much you think *you* oughta be doin'.

REICH: *A lot, don't you think?*

Yeah, but I don't think you should be getting crazy about it. Myself, I do a lot of stuff but a lot of times I don't think I should be; a lot of times I think that I'm just working for the sake of being working; but the thing that happens—a real neat thing that happens—is that if you're working along on energy that's weird, coming from a weird place, you go a certain amount of way but you don't accomplish anything and that's the way you know that you're doing something wrong, just by that sense of non-accomplishment, or the stuff not clicking. But as long as you're doing the right kind of stuff, it's gonna just keep working.

A LONG TIME AGO PEOPLE DECIDED TO LIVE IN AMERICA

Richard Brautigan

Few of the psychedelic writers of the Sixties have been held in greater affection than Richard Brautigan (1935–1984), the warm-hearted, hulking, moustachioed hippy writer and poet, of whom his fans said 'he could cut through the intellectual and emotional noise to touch us all'. Brautigan, who was born in Tacoma, Washington, published his first collections of verse in San Francisco in the late Fifties and modestly described himself as 'a minor poet', although his works were uniformly rich and satisfying and appreciated. Completely at home on the Bay, he became a close friend of Lawrence Ferlinghetti who published a number of his poems and stories in his collections. Brautigan's work was often comic, such as 'Attila at the Gates of the Telephone Company', and occasionally very short, like the single-line 'A 48-year-old Burglar from San Diego'. His affinity with the drug culture was evident in his first novel, A Confederate General from Big Sur, *published in America in 1964, but not until 1971 in Britain. Later books also revealed his versatility with the western, horror and private eye genres, even if they were shot through with his irony and wit and fancy for hallucinatory drugs.*

'A Long Time Ago People Decided to Live in America' is one of a small group of Brautigan's tales, including 'Homage to the San Francisco YMCA' and 'The Betrayed Kingdom', which record the end of the psychedelic era of love and sex and drugs that was signalled by the violence at Altamont in 1969. The Seventies, in fact, would not be the same for him or many others who had revelled in the freedom of the Sixties, and this story

provides a poignant finale to the collection. In the Seventies, Richard Brautigan produced only two more collections of poetry, five novels and a recording, Listening to Richard Brautigan. *Tragically, in September 1984 he took his own life.*

*   *   *

It's dope. It's dope. Mamma warned me against it. My minister said it would rot the bones in my brain cells. My papa put me over his knee and said, 'Stop turning the barnyard stock on, son. One of the cows laid an egg this morning and one of the rabbits tried to put a saddle on.' Ah, dope!

A Confederate General from Big Sur, 1964

I'm wandering along, thinking about how I'd like to get laid by somebody new. It's a cold winter afternoon and just another thought, almost out of my mind when—

A tall, God-I-love-the-tall-ones girl comes walking up the street, casual as a young animal with Levi's on. She must be 5-9, wearing a blue sweater. Her breasts are loose beneath it and move in firm youthful tide.

She has no shoes on.

She's a hippie girl.

Her hair is long.

She doesn't know how pretty she is. I like that. It always turns me on, which isn't very hard to do right now because I'm already thinking about girls.

Then as we pass each other she turns towards me, a thing totally unexpected, and she says, 'Don't I know you?'

Wow! She is standing beside me now. She's really tall!

I look closely at her. I try to see if I know her. Maybe she's a former lover or somebody else I've met or made a pass at when I've been drunk. I look carefully at her and she is beautiful in a fresh young way. She has the nicest blue eyes, but I don't recognise her.

'I know I've seen you before,' she says, looking up into my face. 'What's your name?'

'Clarence.'

'Clarence?'

'Yeah, Clarence.'

'Oh, then I don't know you,' she says.

That was kind of fast.

Her feet are cold on the pavement and she's hunched in a cold-like way towards me.

'What is your name?' I ask, maybe I'm going to make a pass at her. That's what I should be doing right now. Actually, I'm about thirty seconds late in doing it.

'Willow Woman,' she says. 'I'm trying to get out to the Haight-Ashbury. I just got into town from Spokane.'

'I wouldn't,' I say. 'It's very bad out there.'

'I have friends in the Haight-Ashbury,' she says.

'It's a bad place,' I say.

She shrugs her shoulders and looks helplessly down at her feet. Then she looks up and her eyes have a friendly wounded expression in them.

'This is all I have,' she says.

(Meaning what she is wearing.)

'And what's in my pocket,' she says.

(Her eyes glance furtively towards the left rear pocket of her Levi's.)

'My friends will help me out when I get there,' she says.

(Glancing in the direction of the Haight-Ashbury three miles away.)

Suddenly she has become awkward. She doesn't know exactly what to do. She has taken two steps backwards. They are in the direction of going up the street.

'I . . .,' she says.

'I . . .,' looking down at her cold feet again.

She takes another half-step backwards.

'I.'

'I don't want to whine,' she says.

She's really disgusted with what's happening now. She's ready to leave. It didn't work out the way she wanted.

'Let me help you,' I say.

I reach into my pocket.

She steps towards me, instantly relieved as if a miracle has happened.

I give her a dollar, having totally lost somewhere the thread of making a pass at her, which I had planned on doing.

She can't believe it's a dollar and throws her arms around me and kisses me on the cheek. Her body is warm, friendly and giving.

We could make a nice scene together. I could say the words that would cause it to be, but I don't say anything because I've lost the thread of making a pass at her and don't know where it's gone, and she departs beautifully towards all the people that she will ever meet, at best I will turn out to be a phantom memory, and all the lives that she will live.

We've finished living this one together.

She's gone.

Epilogue
A VISIONARY PREDICTION

Aldous Huxley

If the writers in this book can be considered as 'a signpost to new space', then there is one man whom the description fits most perfectly of all: Aldous Huxley (1894–1963). To conclude this collection the following essay, by one of the most revered figures in drug literature, presents the most logical guide to possible new paths for linking drugs and creativity. Huxley was among the pioneer writers on the mescaline experience, and from the sensations he underwent on a spring morning in 1953 when he swallowed four-tenths of a gramme of mescaline dissolved in a glass of water, came those now-classic essays 'The Doors of Perception' (1954) and 'Heaven and Hell' (1956). The impact of Huxley's work—he came from a family of distinguished intellectual background and had completed a brilliant education before taking to writing fiction, journalism and criticism—was enormous, and many who might have scoffed at a lesser man were forced to take notice of his experiences and proposals. Huxley was quite clearly aware of the risks inherent in the drugs he used and this was always in the forefront of his thinking. The following prediction of the future of 'psycho-chemicals' was written shortly before his death for a special symposium conducted by English and American writers on drugs; it is not only a reasoned projection of what might be in store, but a fitting epitaph to a man whose work made so much of what it compounded possible. It is recorded that Huxley took LSD while on his deathbed, and one can only conjecture at what he must have experienced on this unique occasion.

*   *   *

The best vision-inducing art is produced by men and women who have
themselves had the visionary experience; but it is also possible for any
reasonably good artist, simply by following an approved recipe, to create
works which shall have at least some transporting power.

'The Doors of Perception', 1954

Between culture and the individual the relationship is, and always
has been, strangely ambivalent. We are at once the beneficiaries
of our culture and its victims. Without culture, and without that
precondition of all culture, language, man would be no more than
another species of baboon. It is to language and culture that we
owe our humanity. And 'What a piece of work is a man!' says
Hamlet: 'How noble in reason! how infinite in faculties! . . . in
action how like an angel! in apprehension, how like a god!'
But, alas, in the intervals of being noble, rational and potentially
infinite,

> man, proud man,
> Dressed in a little brief authority,
> Most ignorant of what he is most assured,
> His glassy essence, like an angry ape,
> Plays such fantastic tricks before high heaven
> As make the angels weep.

Genius and angry ape, player of fantastic tricks and godlike
reasoner—in all these roles individuals are the products of a
language and a culture. Working on the twelve or thirteen billion
neurons of a human brain, language and culture have given us
law, science, ethics, philosophy; have made possible all the
achievements of talent and of sanctity. They have also given us
fanaticism, superstition and dogmatic bumptiousness; nationalis-
tic idolatry and mass murder in the name of God; rabble-rousing
propaganda and organised lying. And, along with the salt of the
earth, they have given us, generation after generation, countless

millions of hypnotised conformists, the predestined victims of power-hungry rulers who are themselves the victims of all that is most senseless and inhuman in their cultural tradition.

Thanks to language and culture, human behaviour can be incomparably more intelligent, more original, creative and flexible than the behaviour of animals, whose brains are too small to accommodate the number of neurons necessary for the invention of language and the transmission of accumulated knowledge. But, thanks again to language and culture, human beings often behave with a stupidity, a lack of realism, a total inappropriateness, of which animals are incapable.

Trobriand Islander or Bostonian, Sicilian Catholic or Japanese Buddhist, each of us is born into some culture and passes his life within its confines. Between every human consciousness and the rest of the world stands an invisible fence, a network of traditional thinking-and-feeling patterns, of secondhand notions that have turned into axioms, of ancient slogans revered as divine revelations. What we see through the meshes of this net is never, of course, the unknowable 'thing in itself'. It is not even, in most cases, the thing as it impinges upon our senses and as our organism spontaneously reacts to it. What we ordinarily take in and respond to is a curious mixture of immediate experience with culturally conditioned symbols, of sense impressions with preconceived ideas about the nature of things. And by most people the symbolic elements in this cocktail of awareness are felt to be more important than the elements contributed by immediate experience. Inevitably so, for, to those who accept their culture totally and uncritically, words in the familiar language do not stand (however inadequately) for things. On the contrary, things stand for familiar words. Each unique event of their ongoing life is instantly and automatically classified as yet another concrete illustration of one of the verbalised, culture-hallowed abstractions drummed into their heads by childhood conditioning.

It goes without saying that many of the ideas handed down to us by the transmitters of culture are eminently sensible and realistic. (If they were not, the human species would now be extinct.) But, along with these useful concepts, every culture hands down a stock of unrealistic notions, some of which never made any sense, while others may once have possessed survival value, but have now, in the changed and changing circumstances of ongoing history, become completely irrelevant. Since human beings respond to symbols as promptly and unequivocally as they respond to the stimuli of unmediated experience, and since most of them naïvely believe that culture-hallowed words about things are as real as, or even realer than their perceptions of the things themselves, these outdated or intrinsically nonsensical notions do enormous harm. Thanks to the realistic ideas handed down by culture, mankind has survived and, in certain fields, progresses. But thanks to the pernicious nonsense drummed into every individual in the course of his acculturation, mankind, though surviving and progressing, has always been in trouble. History is the record, among other things, of the fantastic and generally fiendish tricks played upon itself by culture-maddened humanity. And the hideous game goes on.

What can, and what should, the individual do to improve his ironically equivocal relationship with the culture in which he finds himself embedded? How can he continue to enjoy the benefits of culture without, at the same time, being stupefied or frenziedly intoxicated by its poisons? How can he become discriminatingly acculturated, rejecting what is silly or downright evil in his conditioning, and holding fast to that which makes for humane and intelligent behaviour?

A culture cannot be discriminatingly accepted, much less be modified, except by persons who have seen through it—by persons who have cut holes in the confining stockade of verbalised symbols and so are able to look at the world and, by reflection, at themselves in a new and relatively unprejudiced way. Such persons are not merely born; they must also be made. But how?

In the field of formal education, what the would-be hole cutter needs is knowledge. Knowledge of the past and present history of cultures in all their fantastic variety, and knowledge about the nature and limitations, the uses and abuses, of language. A man who knows that there have been many cultures, and that each culture claims to be the best and truest of all, will find it hard to take too seriously the boastings and dogmatisings of his own tradition. Similarly, a man who knows how symbols are related to experience, and who practises the kind of linguistic self-control taught by the exponents of General Semantics, is unlikely to take too seriously the absurd or dangerous nonsense that, within every culture, passes for philosophy, practical wisdom and political argument.

As a preparation for hole cutting, this kind of intellectual education is certainly valuable, but no less certainly insufficient. Training on the verbal level needs to be supplemented by training in wordless experiencing. We must learn how to be mentally silent, must cultivate the art of pure receptivity.

To be silently receptive—how childishly simple that seems! But in fact, as we very soon discover, how difficult! The universe in which men pass their lives is the creation of what Indian philosophy calls *Nama-Rupa*, Name and Form. Reality is a continuum, a fathomlessly mysterious and infinite Something, whose outward aspect is what we call Matter and whose inwardness is what we call Mind. Language is a device for taking the mystery out of Reality and making it amenable to human comprehension and manipulation. Acculturated man breaks up the continuum, attaches labels to a few of the fragments, projects the labels into the outside world and thus creates for himself an all-too-human universe of separate objects, each of which is merely the embodiment of a name, a particular illustration of some traditional abstraction. What we perceive takes on the pattern of the conceptual lattice through which it has been filtered. Pure receptivity is difficult because man's normal waking consciousness is always culturally conditioned. But normal waking consciousness, as William James pointed out many years ago, 'is but one type of consciousness, while all about it, parted from it by the filmiest of screens, there lie potential forms of consciousness entirely different. We may go through life without suspecting their existence; but apply the requisite stimulus, and at a touch they are there in all their completeness, definite types of mentality which probably somewhere have their field of application and adaptation. No account of the universe in its totality can be final which leaves these forms of consciousness disregarded.'

Like the culture of which it is conditioned, normal waking consciousness is at once our best friend and a most dangerous enemy. It helps us to survive and make progress; but at the same time it prevents us from actualising some of our most valuable potentialities and, on occasion, gets us into all kinds of trouble. To become fully human, man, proud man, the player of fantastic tricks, must learn to get out of his own way; only then will his infinite faculties and angelic apprehension get a chance of coming to the surface. In Blake's words, we must 'cleanse the doors of perception'; for when the doors of perception are cleansed, 'everything appears to man as it is—infinite.' To normal waking consciousness things are the strictly finite and insulated embodiments of verbal labels. How can we break the habit of automatically imposing our prejudices and the memory of culture-hallowed words upon immediate experience? Answer: by the practice of pure receptivity and mental silence. These will cleanse the doors of perception and, in the process, make possible the emergence of other than normal forms of consciousness— aesthetic consciousness, visionary consciousness, mystical consciousness. Thanks to culture we are the heirs to vast accumulations of knowledge, to a priceless treasure of logic and scientific method, to thousands upon thousands of useful pieces of technological and organisational know-how. But the human mind-body possesses other sources of information, makes use of other types of reasoning, is gifted with an intrinsic wisdom that is independent of cultural conditioning.

Wordsworth writes that 'our meddling intellect [that part of the mind which uses language to take the mystery out of Reality] misshapes the beauteous forms of things: we murder to dissect.' Needless to say, we cannot get along without our meddling intellect. Verbalised conceptual thinking is indispensable. But even when they are used well, verbalised concepts misshape 'the beauteous forms of things'. And when (as happens so often) they are used badly, they misshape our lives by rationalising ancient stupidities, by instigating mass murder, persecution and the playing of all the other fantastically ugly tricks that make the angels weep. Wise nonverbal passiveness is an antidote to unwise verbal activity and a necessary corrective to wise verbal activity. Verbalised concepts about experience used to be supplemented by direct, unmediated acquaintance with events as they present themselves to us.

It is the old story of the letter and spirit. The letter is necessary, but must never be taken too seriously; for, divorced from the spirit, it cramps and finally kills. As for the spirit, it 'bloweth where it listeth' and, if we fail to consult the best cultural charts, we may be blown off our course and suffer shipwreck. At present most of us make the worst of both worlds. Ignoring the freely blowing winds of the spirit and relying on cultural maps which may be centuries out-of-date, we rush full speed ahead under the high-pressure steam of our own overweening self-confidence. The tickets we have sold ourselves assure us that our destination is some port in the Islands of the Blest. In fact it turns out, more often than not, to be Devil's Island.

Self-education on the nonverbal level is as old as civilisation. 'Be still and know that I am God' —for the visionaries and mystics of every time and every place, this has been the first and greatest of the commandments. Poets listen to their Muse and in the same way the visionary and the mystic wait upon inspiration in a state of wise passiveness, of dynamic vacuity. In the Western tradition this state is called 'the prayer of simple regard'. At the other end of the world it is described in terms that are psychological rather than theistic. 'In mental silence we look into our own Self-Nature', we 'hold fast to the Not-Thought which lies in thought', we 'become that which essentially we have always been'. By wise activity we can acquire useful analytical knowledge about the world, knowledge that can be communicated by means of verbal symbols. In the state of wise passiveness we make possible the emergence of forms of consciousness other than the utilitarian consciousness of normal waking life. Useful analytical knowledge about the world is replaced by some kind of biologically inessential but spiritually enlightening acquaintance with the world as beauty. Or there can be direct acquaintance with the intrinsic strangeness of existence, its wild implausibility. And finally there can be direct acquaintance with the world's unity. This immediate mystical experience of being at one with the fundamental Oneness that manifests itself in the infinite diversity of things and minds, can never be adequately expressed in words. Like visionary experience, the experience of the mystic can be talked about only from the outside. Verbal symbols can never convey its inwardness.

It is through mental silence and the practice of wise passiveness that artists, visionaries and mystics have made themselves ready for the immediate experience of the world as beauty, as mystery and as unity. But silence and wise passiveness are not the only roads leading out of the all-too-human universe created by normal, culture-conditioned consciousness. In *Expostulation and Reply*, Wordsworth's bookish friend, Matthew, reproaches the poet because

> You look round in your Mother Earth,
> As if she for no purpose bore you;
> As if you were her first-born birth,
> And none had lived before you!

From the point of view of normal waking consciousness, this is sheer intellectual delinquency. But it is what the artist, the visionary and the mystic must do, and, in fact, have always done. 'Look at a person, a landscape, any common object, as though you were seeing it for the first time.' This is one of the exercises in immediate, unverbalised awareness prescribed in the ancient texts of Tantric Buddhism. Artists, visionaries and mystics refuse to be enslaved to the culture-conditioned habits of feeling, thought and action which their society regards as right and natural. Whenever this seems desirable, they deliberately refrain from projecting upon reality those hallowed word patterns with which all human minds are so copiously stocked. They know as well as anyone else that culture and the language in which any given culture is rooted, are absolutely necessary and that, without them, the individual would not be human. But more vividly than the rest of mankind they also know that, to be *fully* human, the individual must learn to decondition himself, must be able to cut holes in the fence of verbalised symbols that hems him in.

In the exploration of the vast and mysterious world of human potentialities the great artists, visionaries and mystics have been trail-blazing pioneers. But where they have been, others can follow. Potentially, all of us are 'infinite in faculties and like gods in apprehension'. Modes of consciousness different from normal waking consciousness are within the reach of anyone who knows how to apply the necessary stimuli. The universe in which a human being lives can be transfigured into a new creation. We have only to cut a hole in the fence and look around us with what the philosopher, Plotinus, describes as 'that other kind of seeing, which everyone has but few make use of'.

Within our current systems of education, training on the non-verbal level is meagre in quantity and poor in quality. Moreover, its purpose, which is simply to help its recipients to be more 'like gods in apprehension', is neither clearly stated nor consistently pursued. We could and, most emphatically, we should do better in this very important field than we are doing now. The practical wisdom of earlier civilisations and the findings of adventurous spirits within our own tradition and in our own time are freely available. With their aid a curriculum and a methodology of non-verbal training could be worked out without much difficulty. Unhappily most persons in authority have a vested interest in the maintenance of cultural fences. They frown upon hole cutting as subversive and dismiss Plotinus' 'other kind of seeing' as a symptom of mental derangement. If an effective system of nonverbal education could be worked out, would the authorities allow it to be widely applied? It is an open question.

From the nonverbal world of culturally uncontaminated consciousness we pass to the subverbal world of physiology and biochemistry. A human being is a temperament and a product of cultural conditioning; he is also, and primarily, an extremely complex and delicate biochemical system, whose inwardness, as the system changes from one state of equilibrium to another, is changing consciousness. It is because each one of us is a biochemical system that (according to Houseman)

Malt does more than Milton can
To justify God's ways to man.

Beer achieves its theological triumphs because, in William James'
words, 'Drunkenness is the great exciter of the *Yes* function in
man.' And he adds that 'It is part of the deeper mystery and
tragedy of life that whiffs and gleams of something that we
immediately recognise as excellent should be vouchsafed to so
many of us only in the fleeting earlier phases of what, in its
totality, is so degrading a poisoning.' The tree is known by its
fruits, and the fruits of too much reliance upon ethyl alcohol as
an exciter of the *Yes* function are bitter indeed. No less bitter are
the fruits of reliance upon such habit-forming sedatives,
hallucinogens and mood elevators as opium and its derivatives,
as cocaine (once so blithely recommended to his friends and
patients by Dr Freud), as the barbiturates and amphetamine. But
in recent years the pharmacologists have extracted or synthesised
several compounds that powerfully affect the mind without doing
any harm to the body, either at the time of ingestion or, through
addiction, later on. Through these new psychedelics, the subject's
normal waking consciousness may be modified in many different
ways. It is as though, for each individual, his deeper self decides
which kind of experience will be most advantageous. Having
decided, it makes use of the drug's mind-changing powers to
give the person what he needs. Thus, if it would be good for
him to have deeply buried memories uncovered, deeply buried
memories will duly be uncovered. In cases where this is of no
great importance, something else will happen. Normal waking
consciousness may be replaced by aesthetic consciousness, and
the world will be perceived in all its unimaginable beauty, all
the blazing intensity of its 'thereness'. And aesthetic consciousness may modulate into visionary consciousness. Thanks to yet
another kind of seeing, the world will now reveal itself as not
only unimaginably beautiful, but also fathomlessly mysterious—
as a multitudinous abyss of possibility forever actualising itself
into unprecedented forms. New insights into a new, transfigured
world of givenness, new combinations of thought and fantasy—

the stream of novelty pours through the world in a torrent, whose
every drop is charged with meaning. There are the symbols whose
meaning lies outside themselves in the given facts of visionary
experience, and there are these given facts which signify only
themselves. But 'only themselves' is also 'no less than the divine
ground of all being'. 'Nothing but this' is at the same time 'the
Suchness of all'. And now the aesthetic and the visionary consciousness deepen into mystical consciousness. The world is now
seen as an infinite diversity that is yet a unity, and the beholder
experiences himself as being at one with the infinite Oneness that
manifests itself, totally present, at every point of space, at every
instant in the flux of perpetual perishing and perpetual renewal.
Our normal word-conditioned consciousness creates a universe
of sharp distinctions, black and white, this and that, me and you
and it. In the mystical consciousness of being at one with infinite
Oneness, there is a reconciliation of opposites, a perception of
the Not-Particular in particulars, a transcending of our ingrained
subject-object relationships with things and persons; there is an
immediate experience of our solidarity with all beings and a kind
of organic conviction that in spite of the inscrutabilities of fate,
in spite of our own dark stupidities and deliberate malevolence,
yes, in spite of all that is so manifestly wrong with the world, it
is yet, in some profound, paradoxical and entirely inexpressible
way, All Right. For normal waking consciousness, the phrase,
'God is Love', is no more than a piece of wishful positive thinking. For the mystical consciousness, it is a self-evident truth.

Unprecedentedly rapid technological and demographic changes
are steadily increasing the dangers by which we are surrounded,
and at the same time are steadily diminishing the relevance of
the traditional feeling-and-behaviour-patterns imposed upon all
individuals, rulers and ruled alike, by their culture. Always desirable, widespread training in the art of cutting holes in cultural
fences is now the most urgent of necessities. Can such a training
be speeded up and made more effective by a judicious use of the
physically harmless psychedelics now available? On the basis of
personal experience and the published evidence, I believe that it
can. In my utopian fantasy, *Island*, I speculated in fictional terms

about the ways in which a substance akin to psilocybin could be used to potentiate the nonverbal education of adolescents and to remind adults that the real world is very different from the mis-shapen universe they have created for themselves by means of their culture-conditioned prejudices. 'Having Fun with Fungi' — that was how one waggish reviewer dismissed the matter. But which is better: to have Fun with Fungi or to have Idiocy with Ideology, to have Wars because of Words, to have Tomorrow's Misdeeds out of Yesterday's Miscreeds?

How should the psychedelics be administered? Under what circumstances, with what kind of preparation and follow-up? These are questions that must be answered empirically, by large-scale experiment. Man's collective mind has a high degree of viscosity and flows from one position to another with the reluctant deliberation of an ebbing tide of sludge. But in a world of explosive population increase, of headlong technological advance and of militant nationalism, the time at our disposal is strictly limited. We must discover, and discover very soon, new energy sources for overcoming our society's psychological inertia, better solvents for liquefying the sludgy stickiness of an anachronistic state of mind. On the verbal level an education in the nature and limita-tions, the uses and abuses of language; on the wordless level an education in mental silence and pure receptivity; and finally, through the use of harmless psychedelics, a course of chemically triggered conversion experiences or ecstasies—these, I believe, will provide all the sources of mental energy, all the solvents of conceptual sludge, that an individual requires. With their aid, he should be able to adapt himself selectively to his culture, rejecting its evils, stupidities and irrelevancies, gratefully accepting all its treasures of accumulated knowledge, of rationality, human-heartedness and practical wisdom. If the number of such indi-viduals is sufficiently great, if their quality is sufficiently high, they may be able to pass from discriminating acceptance of their culture to discriminating change and reform. Is this a hopefully utopian dream? Experiment can give us the answer, for the dream is prag-matic; the utopian hypotheses can be tested empirically. And in these oppressive times a little hope is surely no unwelcome visitant.

ACKNOWLEDGEMENTS

This is a revised and updated edition of my book *The Hashish Club—An Anthology of Drug Literature, Volume Two: The Psychedelic Era*, first published in 1975, and I would like to record my thanks to my publisher, Ernest Hecht, for his foresight in seeing that now is the time to republish the work. I am also grateful to Dan Franklin and Tessa Harrow, my editors on the two editions, and to Lawrence Ferlinghetti, Brian W. Aldiss, and the late Terry Southern and Alexander Trocchi, all of whom were generous with their help and suggestions during my original research for the book in the Seventies. The publishers and I also thank the following writers, agents and publishers for permission to include the various stories and extracts in this collection: City Lights Publishing Co., Inc. of San Francisco for the poem 'This is the Powerful Knowledge' by Michael McClure; 'The Tape' from *Visions of Cody* by Jack Kerouac and the extract from *The First Third* by Neal Cassady; the extract from 'Essay' and 'Writing Dreams' from *Book of Dreams* by Jack Kerouac; 'Letter to Timothy Leary' and 'I Am Dying, Meester?' from *The Yage Letters* by William S. Burroughs and Allen Ginsberg; 'The Great Being' by Allen Ginsberg; the extracts from 'Elegiac Feelings American' (*Contemporary Poets*) and *The American Express* by Gregory Corso; the extract from *Starting from San Francisco* and 'Where is Vietnam?' by Lawrence Ferlinghetti. Also Farrar, Straus & Giroux, Inc. for two extracts from *The Electric Kool-Aid Acid Test* by Tom Wolfe; New American Library, Inc., New York, for 'LSD is Air' by Timothy Leary; Random Publishing Group for the extracts from *In My Own Way* and *The Joyous*

Cosmology by Alan Watts, 'Neville Club' from *In His Own Write* by John Lennon, and the extract from *A Confederate General from Big Sur* and 'A Long Time Ago People Decided to Live in America' from *Revenge of the Lawn* by Richard Brautigan; Doubleday & Co., Inc., New York, for the three extracts including 'Good Ole Cagey Cage' from *Be Not Content* by William J. Craddock and the extract from *The Storming of the Mind* by Robert Hunter; Houghton Mifflin Publishers, New York, for the extract and 'A Trip to Stonesville' from *The Natural Mind* by Andrew Weil; Avon Books, New York, for the extract from *The Teachings of Don Juan: A Yaqui Way of Knowledge* by Carlos Castaneda; Peter Owen Ltd. for the extract from 'The Story of Lahcen and Idir' and 'The Wind at Beni Midar' by Paul Bowles; New Directions, New York, for the extract from *Epreuves, Exorcismes* and 'My King' from *La Nuit Remue* by Henri Michaux; Sterling Lord Literistic, Inc. for the extract from *Red Dirt Marijuana* and 'The Blood of a Wig' by Terry Southern; Christopher Logue and the Estate of Alexander Trocchi for the extract from *Cain's Book* and 'The Long Book' by Alexander Trocchi; John Calder Ltd. for the extract from *The Process* and 'Let The Mice In' from *The Third Mind* by Brion Gysin and William S. Burroughs; Straight Arrow Books, Inc. and *Rolling Stone* for the quotes by Bob Dylan, John Lennon (*Lennon Remembers*), Hunter S. Thompson and the extract from *A Signpost to New Space* and 'A Conscious Tool of the Universe' by Jerry Garcia, Charles Reich and Jann Wenner; Abner Stein Literary Agency for the extract from *Fear and Loathing in Las Vegas* by Hunter S. Thompson; Spice Box Books, Inc., San Francisco, for the extract from *Smokestack El Ropo's Bedside Reader* and 'Fable the Third' by Smokestack El Ropo; Curtis Brown Group Ltd. for the extract from *The Doors of Perception* and 'A Visionary Prediction' by Aldous Huxley. Finally, I should like to acknowledge the following publications for the use of quotations from their pages: *The Times*, *The New Yorker*, *The New York Herald Tribune*, *Time*, *Evergreen Review* and *Playboy* magazine.